Perfect Warriors

Touchdown Tony Butkovich and the 1943 Purdue Football Team

Cory Palm

Foreword by Ryan Kerrigan

Copyright © 2022 Cory Palm

All rights reserved.

ISBN: 9798799178109

DEDICATION

For Jaclyn and Alyssa…you are the reason I do all that I do. Each day I wake up, I aim to make you as happy as you make me and know that I can't come close.

CONTENTS

	Foreword by Ryan Kerrigan	 i
1	The Battle Before the War	 1
2	A University at War	 9
3	The Navy's V-12 Program	 16
4	Concerns on Campus	 23
5	The Men Who Would Lead Them	 29
6	The Boys on the Team	 36
7	The Season Begins	 46
8	Week 2 | at Marquette	 56
9	Week 3 | vs. Illinois	 62
10	Week 4 | vs. Camp Grant	 72
11	Week 5 | vs. Ohio State in Cleveland	 95
12	Week 6 | vs. Iowa	 103
13	Week 7 | at Wisconsin	 112
14	Week 8 | at Minnesota	 120
15	Week 9 | at Indiana	 127
16	After the Season: The Coaches	 139
17	After the Season: The Players	 148
18	After the Season: The Purd-Illini	 159
19	Touchdown Tony	 171
	Afterword	 176

ACKNOWLEDGMENTS

As with any undertaking, this project could not have happened without many important people. Purdue Athletics was very generous in the use of their archives and helping this project move forward. A special thank you to Tanner Lipsett, Rachel Coe and Matthew Staudt for always being my sounding board on ideas great and small, whether they had the time and interest or not. And to Marcia Iles, for whom the words don't exist for me to explain my gratitude for all you do for me on a daily basis.

Thank you to Ryan Kerrigan for choosing to be a small part of this project. I hope it makes you as proud as you've made us all of these years.

Special thanks are in order for my family as well. I am only where I am in life because of my parents, Tom and Sue Palm, and I will forever be grateful for all of their dedication and sacrifice. For my brothers, Ryan and Chad, to whom I owe so much of who I am including my love of history and this unhealthy passion for sports.

Finally, I want to acknowledge the wonderfulness of college athletics. For more than a century, college sports have afforded opportunities to millions who may have had no other way to achieve greatness in life. I pray that these opportunities never go away for there are too many great stories yet to tell.

FOREWORD

By Ryan Kerrigan

I've always had a great deal of respect for history and its ability to teach us about ourselves. Growing up in Muncie, Ind., I was always drawn to sports stories and sports stars that I could connect to. That didn't change when I got to Purdue and had the good fortune to start meeting some of the players I had always looked up to. Guys like Rosevelt Colvin, Drew Brees and Leroy Keyes were part of the reason I came to Purdue. The importance of the legacy they left can't be overstated. I knew I could accomplish anything as a Boilermaker because the men who came before me had laid the foundation for success. And that applies to the 1943 Boilermaker team, those *Perfect Warriors*, ten-fold.

I had heard the names of a few of the men who played on the squad celebrated in this story. A couple of them are still in the Purdue record books and, of course, everyone who comes through Purdue Athletics has heard of Red Mackey and Pinky Newell. But getting to know the team in depth, what an inspiring tale. To know that we shared the same practice fields, walked the same paths to class and existed in the same realm decades apart is humbling. There is nothing like running out on the field of Ross-Ade Stadium in front of die-hard Purdue fans. I know what that feeling is and these men knew it too. I am in awe of what they did at Purdue and beyond.

Purdue means the world to me and always will. The four years I spent in college were the best four years of my life and I cherish the memories and relationships I made on the field and off. Whether it was earning unanimous All-America honors my final year, helping the legendary coach Joe Tiller win his final game or being inducted into the Purdue Intercollegiate Athletics Hall of Fame, I take great pride in what I accomplished at Purdue. I'll never pass on a chance to come back to Ross-Ade and "Shout!" with the fans. But to have added to the legacy of all of the great Boilermakers that came before me, to have contributed to a history that includes Tony Butkovich, Alex Agase, Dick Barwegen and the rest of these *Perfect Warriors* truly means the world to me.

CHAPTER 1

THE BATTLE BEFORE THE WAR

They came from all over, to meet in Chicago, these temporary Boilermakers seeking perfection. See, the students were on a break from the university as Purdue had just completed the fall term, with a group of graduating seniors finishing up their autumnal coursework. The entire student body had been dismissed from campus on Wednesday, Oct. 27, with the winter session not scheduled to begin until the following Thursday, Nov. 4, 1943. And although they were a part of the student body and yet a separate entity on their own, the Navy V-12 students on campus had received a leave that corresponded with the fall break. This leave was vital, as the end of the fall term represented something completely different to the future Naval officers. While their civilian classmates were relaxing and getting ready for their winter coursework, a large portion of the V-12 students were facing a trip to basic training followed by deployment overseas.

They had come to Purdue University in July 1943, more than 1,250 strong, to study and train, preparing to become Naval officers. The need for officers was immense with the country in a titanic struggle for the soul of the world. The Navy College Training Program had launched just a few months prior, allowing anyone aged 17 to 20 to test their way into the hybrid program, designed to produce officers for the Navy, Marines and Coast Guard. Purdue president Edward C. Elliott had qualified the university in rural Indiana as a "national war training agency" and it lived up to this mission when it was selected as a V-12 institution.[1]

Included in that group of future officers was a talented group of athletes, mostly Marine trainees, sent to Purdue from around the Midwest. It was an interesting group, unprecedented in school history for its makeup. They joined a football program that included precious few current Purdue University students who had competed on the 1942 squad, a team that finished the season with just one win to go with eight losses. That squad, led by first-year coach Elmer Burnham, had scored only 27 points in nine contests, placing eighth in the nine-team conference.[2] Yes, there were a few holdovers on the 1943 squad, though not many. And, truth be told, that may not have been such a terrible thing.

But aside from those returning lettermen, of which there were little more than a dozen, there were plenty of others with experience. It's just that experience didn't come as Boilermakers. Instead the men were Rams from Fordham and Tigers from Missouri. They included Hawkeyes from Iowa and nearly an entire platoon of Fighting Illini from neighboring Illinois. But these men were sailors and Marines first, student-athletes second. In fact, when the 1943 team convened for fall camp in West Lafayette, there were 82 men on the squad. That number included 25 Navy trainees, 46 future Marines and just 11 civilians. They had transferred to West Lafayette, Ind., as members of the officers' training program and, thanks to a special ruling by the Department of the Navy, had been allowed to continue their gridiron careers, despite the unconventional route.

This group included several different types of players. There were a few stars. Guard Alex Agase was an All-American at the University of Illinois as a sophomore in 1942 while his former teammates with the Fighting Illini, John Genis and Mike Kasap, were starting tackles. Agase and Genis immediately endeared themselves to teammates upon arriving in West Lafayette, earning co-captain honors at the outset of the season despite their short tenure with the Boilermakers. In the backfield, starting quarterback Sam Vacanti had played for the University of Iowa in 1942, while halfbacks Stanley Dubicki, Keith

Parker, Lewis Rose and Boris Dimancheff had all starred with their previous schools.[3]

The 1943 season provided this group of men a chance to continue playing a game they enjoyed, even while most were preparing for war. While their training continued for their greatest challenge, the season provided one successful distraction after another. And the wins piled up. As the fall term wound down, a homecoming victory over the University of Iowa gave the Boilermakers a perfect 6-0 record, with just three games to play. Next up was a contest at the University of Wisconsin, followed by matchups against the University of Minnesota and intrastate rival Indiana University.

Then word came that would drastically alter the season. With the end of the fall term and the subsequent graduation of many V-12 trainees, those who were no longer being schooled would be transferred for physical training and then sent to active duty in the Pacific Theatre. This included several hundred of Purdue's V-12 trainees, and it included 13 members of the Boilermakers football squad. Given the situation, head coach Elmer Burnham elected to allow his players the week off leading up to the Wisconsin game. With classes in between sessions and all military personnel on furlough, the football squad scattered as well. The team would convene as a whole on Friday, Oct. 29, at the Edgewater Beach Hotel, on the shores of Lake Michigan.[4]

And so, they came from all over, to meet in Chicago and prepare for the final game of the season as one team. Coach Burnham led the only formal, full squad practice of the week at the Edgewater. It shouldn't have taken much for the nationally ranked Boilermakers to handle Wisconsin. Purdue came into the game ranked fourth in the nation, while the Badgers owned a record of 1-4 on the year, including consecutive losses to Notre Dame and Indiana.

But as the Boilermakers prepared to head to Madison on that Saturday morning, things started to turn for the worse. The train out of Chicago was delayed and the arrival in Madison was pushed back. The Boilermakers were forced to prepare for the contest while on the train as it barreled down the tracks. One car was turned into a locker room, with players getting dressed in jerseys, pads and cleats and all the rest. Another car was converted into a training room, with still more players receiving their pre-game medical treatments and taping of different extremities. Word was passed ahead to the Madison station, notifying them of the urgency of the situation. Taxicabs lined the street when the train finally arrived at the station, ready to whisk the team the final mile from the depot to Camp Randall Stadium for kickoff.[5]

Players piled into the taxicabs, pads and all, and made their way to the stadium. The hour was so late upon arriving at the stadium that there was no time for pregame warmups. It was straight to the coin-toss and kickoff. And, how many things were going against the Boilermakers, it would have been understandable, perhaps, if they had not performed at a peak level. It would have made sense if they had failed to maintain their perfect record. They had precious little preparation throughout the week and virtually none on gameday. They hadn't really stretched or warmed up, being cooped up in a train, as it were. And in the backs of their minds was the thought that this was the final time they would suit up together and for many, perhaps the final time they would ever don a football uniform. Given these handicaps, it would have been understandable if they had lost.

They promptly came out and defeated the Badgers 32-0.

As if the challenge of maintaining the perfect record and sending off the future Marines victorious wasn't enough, something larger was at stake as the contest began. Heading into the game, star fullback Tony Butkovich was closing in on the Big Ten single season scoring record. Coming into the contest in Madison, Butkovich had tallied 10 scores in just three Big Ten games. Everyone knew coming into the showdown with the Badgers that Tony needed to cross the goal line three times for the record. And it would be his final chance, as he was among the Marines scheduled to ship out come Monday.

A fairly pedestrian start of the game didn't lead to much action until the Boilermakers took advantage of the game's first turnover. On the next play, Butkovich scooted around the right end for a 33-yard touchdown and a 6-0 lead. The Purdue fullback scored again late in the second quarter and the Boilermakers took a 13-0 edge into the break. More importantly, "Touchdown Tony" had tied the conference scoring record and, with a half to play, would need just one more point to hold the distinction for himself.

After a sloppy third quarter full of miscues by both sides, the Boilermakers once again found their footing. Late in the third, Boris "Babe" Dimancheff burst through a hole in the left side of the line, shoved a would-be Wisconsin tackler out of the way and sprinted 46 yards to pay dirt. Now ahead 19-0 and with the PAT still pending, Coach Burnham tried to get his star fullback the Big Ten scoring record. After all, who knew if the Boilermakers would get another chance, especially given how unpredictable the game had been so far. Butkovich was assigned the task of drop-kicking the extra point, which would have given him the record. However, Tony had not tried too many kicks in game action and it showed, as the kick went wildly astray. He remained tied for the record and the score stayed at 19-0.[6]

And that's how it stood as the fourth quarter crept along. Following an interception by Purdue defensive back Dick Bushnell, the Boilermakers took possession at their 36-yard line halfway through the final frame. At this point, something quite remarkable happened.

There were more than 10,000 fans in attendance at Camp Randall Stadium that afternoon, enjoying the last weekend in October. The weather was good, but the product on the field was not, as it was now clear their Badgers would be on the losing end once again. These fans had suffered through a difficult season so far, seeing their team win just one game in six to this point. And though they had hung with the fourth-best team in the country for a good portion of the day, seeing their team give up eight turnovers on this day was gut-wrenching. These 10,000 Badger faithful could have left the stadium in disgust, the outcome of the game having long been decided. Instead, nearly the entire crowd remained and began cheering for Butkovich and his mates to break the scoring record for good.[7]

With just five minutes remaining and 64 yards between them and the record, Purdue's offense trotted onto the field for what was likely to be the final time that afternoon. Purdue gave a heavy dose of Butkovich and Dimancheff on the drive. Babe, who would end the game with 15 carries for 111 yards to go with his long scoring run and an interception, carried the ball 14 yards down to the Wisconsin 13-yard line. From here, it would be Butkovich's load to carry, as surely Burnham would not want to chance losing the scoring title for Tony because of another player crossing the goal line.

On the next play, Tony went for no gain. On second down, it was right tackle John Genis leading the way, as Tony made it down to the 3-yard line. Or so it seemed. A holding call nullified the play and the Boilermakers were set back all the way to the 25-yard line. The clock continued to tick off the seconds. At this point, facing second-and-long, the Boilermakers had to take whatever Wisconsin gave them. Well, Wisconsin was loaded up to stop the run. So, Purdue quarterback Sam Vacanti hooked up with end Herb Hoffman for a 25-yard scoring pass. With 3:25 remaining in the game, and the Boilermakers now leading 25-0, Butkovich would once again get a chance at the scoring record via a point-after attempt. But it seemed destined that he would remain tied for the record, as he failed to convert the kick for the second time.

Now Coach Burnham had to make the decision. Should he take drastic measures to get his fullback the record? Trying Butkovich at kicker for the PAT's was one thing, as it was well within the natural flow of the game to trot him out for those attempts. But now, with just three minutes remaining and the game well in hand, Burnham had to decide whether to try an onside kick in an effort to get the ball back one last time. Burnham elected to pull out all the stops and sent reserve tackle Tom Hughes out to try the onside kick. Hughes' kick was perfect as Dimancheff leapt into the air at mid-field to snatch the ball away from a waiting Wisconsin player and give his teammate one last opportunity.

Tony didn't disappoint, breaking the first play of the drive for 15 yards, down to the 35-yard-line. It seemed like the Boilers were getting the breaks they needed and Tony would get the record, much to the crowd's delight. On the very next play, Vacanti attempted a middle screen pass to the fullback. It was intercepted by Wisconsin lineman Joe Keenan. The crowd, despite seeing their defense make one of the best plays of the day, groaned in displeasure.

Wisconsin's offense lost yards on consecutive plays, with a penalty and a run for a loss of six. On third-and-long Vacanti, seeking redemption for throwing a drive-killing interception just moments earlier, stepped in front of a Wisconsin pass and made an interception of his own. Vacanti broke a tackle and had a clear path to the end zone, but he thought better of it. In a play that typified the team-first attitude displayed by Purdue all afternoon, Vacanti slowed up a bit and allowed himself to be tackled at the Wisconsin 5-yard line.[8]

Butkovich would have one last opportunity. On the first play from scrimmage, Tony headed for a hole on the left side of the line and carried three Wisconsin defenders to the goal line, seeming to break the plain of the goal line and the 12-year-old conference scoring record. However, the officials had other ideas and called forward motion dead just inches short of the end zone. Just 29 seconds remained on the clock, though no one was sure of the exact time remaining in the game, as the clock had begun to malfunction at the start of the second half. The scoreboard clock was a mere suggestion at this point as the official timekeeper was the only man in the stadium who truly knew how much time remained.

Vacanti traded positions with his fullback for the next play and Butkovich took the snap directly from center Walt Poremba. However, the play was stopped before it began, as both sides were ruled offside in the scramble. On the next play, Vacanti returned under center and Butkovich headed back to his fullback position. Tony took the handoff and crashed straight up the middle, crossing the goal line and taking the scoring record with his 13th touchdown in just four conference games. For the day, Tony carried the ball 28 times for 147 yards, none were more important than those final three.[9]

The crowd rejoiced at seeing history being made, even if it was made by the opposing team. And now, thanks to getting the record in a conventional way, regular kicker Tom Hughes was able to convert the PAT. Because of the game's frenetic nature and the chaos of the final sequence of plays, no one in the stadium quite knew how close Purdue had come to failing to get the record for Butkovich. They would soon find out. As Hughes came out for the ensuing kickoff, 26 seconds showed on the game clock. However, while the kick was coming to a rest in the end zone, the final gun blasted, ending the contest. On top of the madness of the day and the chaos of the fourth quarter, Butkovich nearly lost his record due to that malfunctioning game clock.[10]

In the end, "Touchdown Tony" got the record and Purdue got the win, improving to a perfect 7-0 on the season. The Boilermaker offense rushed for 258 yards with both Butkovich and Dimancheff breaking the century mark. And the defense, in addition to forcing eight Badger turnovers, held Wisconsin to just 116 yards of total offense.[11]

When the Associated Press poll came out the following week, Purdue had risen to number two in the nation, with two games left to play.[12] Of course, by then the team was drastically different. A third of the traveling squad, 13 players in all, were on their way to Parris

Island, S.C., for basic training. While, the remaining Boilermakers would go on to battle Minnesota and Indiana, their teammates were headed off to war.

CHAPTER 2

A UNIVERSITY AT WAR

Sunday, December 7, 1941, that day of great infamy, hit Purdue University much like it hit the rest of the United States of America. And though it took a little while to figure out exactly what the role of the Indiana's land-grant institution would be, once the dust settled, Purdue was deeply involved in both training individuals and working in a larger manner for the war effort.

The Japanese attack on Pearl Harbor began at just before 8 a.m. local Hawaii time and lasted only a few hours. The fact that it was a Sunday morning played a part in the effectiveness of the attack, but it also helped to slow the transmission of the news to the mainland. Given the five-hour time difference, it was early afternoon in West Lafayette when the first Japanese planes appeared over Pearl Harbor. Word spread slowly on the campus. The student body was nearing the end of the fall term, no doubt looking forward to their Christmas break. Advertisements of local shops filled the newspapers that week, along with stories on the start of the Purdue basketball season, scheduled to begin on December 8 with a game against Wabash College.[1]

But as word of the attack made its way to campus, university leaders began the process of determining the institution's next steps. Professors, staff and students alike were no doubt tuned in to hear President Franklin Roosevelt's declaration of war before Congress on December 8.

"Yesterday, December 7, 1941 – a date which will live in infamy – the United States of America was suddenly and deliberately attacked by naval and air forces of the Empire of Japan," Roosevelt began.[2]

Many on campus listened the next night as well when Roosevelt gave the first of what would become his regular "Fireside Chats" from the White House. In that 25-minute radio address to the nation on Dec. 9, 1941, Roosevelt laid out the case for the war against what he called the "gangsterism" threatening the world in the form of the Axis Powers, namely Japan and Germany. He also spoke of the righteousness of the American cause.

"We are now in the midst of a war, not for conquest, not for vengeance, but for a world in which this nation, and all that this nation represents, will be safe for our children," Roosevelt concluded. "So, we are going to win this war and we are going to win the peace that follows."[3]

* * * * *

While everyone in the Purdue community attempted to figure out their place in the new and dramatically different world, one former Boilermaker had already more than made his mark. George S. Welch came to Purdue in 1937 to study aeronautics and science in large part because of the creation of the university-owned airport earlier that decade. A member of the Delta Upsilon fraternity and the university's ROTC program, Welch was one of the first students to earn his wings through the university's Civil Aeronautics Authority (CAA) accredited program. In 1940, nearing his graduation date, Welch decided to drop out of school and join the United State Army Air Corps. Welch finished his training and was given his first commission, at Hamilton Field in San Rafael, Calif. Shortly after arriving in California, Welch was transferred to Wheeler Air Field in Hawaii, assigned to 47th Fighter Squadron, 18th Fighter Group.[4]

It was there that, on the morning of the attacks, Welch found himself able to put his training and education to good use. On the evening of Dec. 6, 1941, Welch attended a formal dinner that ended with an all-night poker game. As the sun broke over the Pacific, Welch and his wingman, Lt. Ken Taylor, were still dressed in their tuxedo slacks from the party as the first wave of Japanese planes attacked. Welch and Taylor called ahead to the Haleiwa Air Strip to have their P-40s readied immediately. A training exercise had caused Welch to move his plane to the auxiliary site, which saved it from being damaged during the first wave of the attack on Wheeler Field. After calling ahead to the Haleiwa Air Field, the two pilots then headed to Taylor's new Buick and raced to the air strip on the north shore of Oahu.[5]

With the Japanese in full assault, Welch and Taylor were able to launch and take on the enemy. In the ensuing action, Welch shot down four Japanese planes, while Taylor shot down three. A little over a week after the attack, Welch gave an interview to the Associated Press recounting the events of that fateful day. "All hell broke loose before I knew it," he said from his base in Honolulu. "I picked the nearest one and went after him. I blazed away but nothing seemed to happen at first, but I got a good bead on him and the next thing I knew he was going down in flames." [6]

Taylor and Welch sought out more targets but soon realized they were low on ammunition. Both men returned to the air field at Haleiwa to reload and then continued their defense of the homeland. Taylor was eventually wounded and had to call off the counter-attack. Welch didn't know until he landed how close he'd come to disaster.

"When I came back to the field I had three bullet holes in my ship, one in the propeller, one in the motor and another just behind the pilot's seat," he said.[7]

For their actions, Welch and Taylor were nominated for the Medal of Honor. They were denied this honor because they had officially taken off without orders to do so.[8] However, both were eventually awarded the Distinguished Service Cross, with Welch presented his honor by President Franklin Roosevelt at the White House in a ceremony with his parents in attendance.[9]

Following the Battle of Pearl Harbor, Welch remained in the Pacific Theatre, recording a total of 16 Japanese kills in more than 300 missions, making him among the most accomplished flying aces of World War II. He served a total of three combat tours and eventually was knocked out of the fighting, not by a Japanese Zero but by a case of malaria. Welch left the Army Air Corps in 1944 and became a test pilot for North American Aviation in California.[10]

He spent the next decade as one of the premiere test pilots in the world. In October 1954, Welch was on a test flight of the F100-A, a supersonic jet fighter. A problem in flight led to a spectacular crash from which Welch would not recover. He died while being transported to the hospital. The life of the great aviator was cut short.[11] But in 1941, on that early December morning in Hawaii, this former Boilermaker made his mark, getting into the fight and exemplifying the American spirit that would not rest until victory was attained.

*　　*　　*　　*　　*

Back on campus, university president Edward C. Elliott addressed the community in an open letter to the university and the greater Lafayette area. In this missive, Elliott made clear that although the future was uncertain, the student body had to live up to its responsibilities. "Now is the time to furnish proof of our unity and our loyalty," wrote Elliott. "Until it is known just what your new duties are to be, your exclusive business is to tend strictly to your business as students…You will show good sense by not being too impatient, but by waiting for the proper advice as to your next duties."[12]

President Elliott also announced a special university convocation on the following Monday, December 15. This event would be the occasion at which Elliott would begin to address the university's place in the war effort.[13] Surely a research-based public institution such as Purdue would play an important role in America's preparedness. But as a school that focused heavily on engineering, Purdue was in a unique position to assist in the effort.

At 11 o'clock on the morning of Dec. 15, an audience of more than 5,000 packed into the Purdue Hall of Music to hear President Elliott and others speak at the convocation, which began with a performance by the Purdue Symphonic Band. After statements by student leaders that called on their peers to be aware of their responsibilities to the nation and themselves, President Elliott addressed the audience.[14]

Elliott spoke directly to two different factions amongst the student body: those who planned to leave school and enlist in the military and those who elected to stay in school and continue their studies. To the first group, Elliott urged them to not take their decision lightly, not to seek adventure and to solicit advice from loved ones. For those who were to remain as civilians, Elliott put forth a five-point bill of responsibilities:

1. As never before, apply yourselves as students.
2. Individually and collectively, to reduce to that minimum requisite your time and your concentration on serious tasks.
3. Aid the University to be economical.
4. Display your true character as a citizen.
5. Maintain your health and physical fitness.

Elliott also called for the creation of a Student War Council to handle student-war relations. The assembly ended with the playing of the "Star-Spangled Banner" and the somber appearance of the nation's colors in a spotlighted fashion above the stage.[15]

And yet, for all the rhetoric, little immediate change was evident on campus. Students were urged to study as usual. After all, there were only a few days remaining until many of these students would be leaving to head home for the holidays. And then just a few days remained in the new year until the end of the semester. But a foundation was laid for the future of the university.

In an editorial on Dec. 9, the university's student newspaper, *The Purdue Exponent,* laid out its "War Platform". In addition to declaring the overall support for the war effort against the Axis powers of Japan, Germany and Italy, the board made specific calls to their peers. Amongst the points made within were that students should "take full advantage of the facilities offered by Purdue" since there would be a great need in the years ahead for men and women trained in the sciences.[16]

When students returned to campus in early January 1942, they were coming back to a vastly different institution. Purdue University had shifted to a war schedule, right down to reconfiguring the academic calendar. The fall semester would conclude as scheduled on January 10, 1942, with the second semester starting less than a week later. Spring break was canceled and the end of the spring semester scheduled for May 2. From there, Purdue would launch into a third term for the academic year, as the university adopted a 12-month, trimester schedule.[17]

At the same time, other measures on campus helped to change the focus of the university. Students involved in the CAA Civilian Pilot Training Program were granted up to 30 hours of flying credit by the Army Air Corps, as both recognition of the training they had already received and incentive to join the Army[18]. Meanwhile, the U.S. Naval Reserve began offering deferments to juniors and seniors, promising to allow the students to finish their schooling before calling them to active duty. The university announced the creation of defense training courses in cities throughout the state. These courses included training in everything from surveying and welding to radio engineering and chemistry. War relief efforts began almost immediately as well, as campus drives began collecting clothes, publications, and other items deemed necessary to aid in the efforts.[19]

One question weighing heavily on the minds of students was the issue of draft deferments. As the spring semester dawned, the university was given an answer on this issue as well. The official word came from the Tippecanoe County selective service board. The dictum, issued by Maj. Howard G. Wade, Occupational Deferment Advisor for the State Selective Service System, stated the criteria under which a deferment would be granted. First of all, the coursework being studied had to be deemed necessary to the war program. In addition, the student was required to attend the university continuously, maintain a 3.5 grade point average, and promise to join the service immediately upon graduation. This effectively made it mandatory for all students who were drafted to attend the new summer session in order to ensure their deferment status, as well as taking school very seriously in order to maintain the high standard of a 3.5 grade index.[20]

That the students were concerned about the draft was a new phenomenon. It was only a few years earlier, in September 1940, that President Franklin Roosevelt signed into law the Selective Service and Training Act of 1940, requiring men who were 26 to 35 years of age to register as eligible for military service. Those drafted were initially bound to 12-months of active duty followed by 10 years spent in reserves or until he reached 45 years of age.[21] It was the first peacetime conscription in American history and the first time the military draft had been instituted since 1920, when it was discontinued following the end of WWI.

In the days and weeks after the attacks at Pearl Harbor and the U.S.'s declaration of war against the Axis powers, thousands flooded military recruiting centers. But seeking strength in numbers, and the reality of fighting a war on two separate fronts, the draft continued. In March 1942, the Selective Service held their first-ever draft for calling men to active duty. More than nine million men were eligible in the first lottery drawing, running from ages 20 to 44.[22] By November 1942, the draft age had been lowered from 20 to 18 and the system changed to draft men in order of age, from oldest to youngest. And as the fighting began, the conscription was changed from 12-months of active duty to last for the duration of the war.[23]

Throughout the course of the war, more than 10 million Americans were drafted into active duty.[24] Of course, following the attack on Pearl Harbor, there was a massive influx of volunteers signing up to join the Army, Navy, Marines and Coast Guard. Because of this influx and the redundancy of having both conscription and volunteerism, in December 1942 President Roosevelt issued an executive order making it impossible to volunteer for service for those between 18 and 37. For the duration of the war, the only way to enlist was to be drafted. One effect this move had was to take control out of the hands of the individual and to allow the War Department to decide where the new personnel would be assigned.[25]

The fact remained, whether they volunteered or were drafted, there was a major influx of new enlisted personnel. With the constant need for evermore soldiers, sailors and Marines, the military was now faced with the reality that they needed men to lead them. This directly led to the creation of additional officer training programs. The Army Specialized Training Program was established and instituted at over 220 colleges and universities around the country.[26] The Navy's V-5 Naval Aviation Cadet program and V-7 Midshipman's School program existed before the war but ramped up in the months after the attack. Both were eventually integrated into a new program the Navy was establishing on college campuses: The V-12 program.[27]

CHAPTER 3

THE NAVY'S V-12 PROGRAM

The early months of 1942 were not a good time for Allied Forces. In Europe, Hitler had spent the previous three years invading and taking control of most of the continent, including Poland in 1939 and Belgium, Holland and France in 1940. By 1941, the European Axis powers had taken control of Northern Africa and most of eastern Europe and began to push east towards the Soviet Union. Meanwhile, half a world away in the Pacific theatre, Japanese forces were on a roll. The attack on Pearl Harbor occurred in conjunction with an attack on U.S. bases in the Philippines, a fight that stretched on for five months before American forces surrendered the island in May 1942. In that same time frame, Japan had victories on Guam, Wake Island and nearly a dozen other strategic locations across the south Pacific.

It wasn't until the American victory in the Battle of Midway in June 1942 that the Allied forces found their footing in the Pacific. That brutal battle saw the Japanese lose four aircraft carriers in the defeat, an incalculable loss that would plague them until the end of the war.[1] The victory at Midway combined with the costly strategic win in the Guadalcanal Campaign taught the Americans a few vital lessons. One was that the tide of the war was turning. With consecutive Allied victories, Japan's seeming invincibility had been shattered.[2] Another lesson, perfectly illustrated by the five-month-long campaign to capture Guadalcanal Canal in "Operation Watchtower", was that this battle was going to be very long and very costly. It was likely to take several years and millions of sailors to accomplish victory.[3]

As such, they would also need a steady supply of young officers to lead those men. The Navy's V-7 program existed prior to the war and served, along with NROTC programs, to provide for college trained commissioned officers. In February 1942, the Navy established the V-1 program for students already in their freshmen or sophomore years in college.[4] Those who entered the V-1 program would accelerate their education, graduate and activate by July 1, 1943. But there was also the impending movement to change the selective service age from 20 to 18. This would make all men 18 and older draft-eligible, severely affecting the supply of college-aged men eligible for these officer training programs. An alternative was needed.

Under the direction of President Roosevelt, the Department of the Navy spent most of 1942 partnering with university presidents from around the country to come up with a roadmap for a college-based program to assist the Navy with the war effort. This suited the nation's educators just fine as they had been working since January 1942 to try and figure a way they could answer the nation's call. More than a thousand representatives from colleges and universities had gathered in Baltimore just weeks after the attack on Pearl Harbor to offer their institutions in service to the country.[5]

After months of negotiations and meetings, on December 12, 1942, the creation of the Army Specialized Training Program (ASTP) and the Navy's V-12 program were announced jointly by the Secretary of War and the Secretary of the Navy.

"The demands of mechanical war and the steadily growing armed forces require a flow into the respective services of young men who require specialized educational technical training which could be provided by the colleges and universities," read the opening paragraph of the official announcement.[6]

Interest amongst the nation's colleges and universities was strong. More than 1,600 schools from around the country, large and small, applied to be a host institution for the V-12 program.[7] And the reasons went beyond patriotic duty. With millions of college-aged men heading overseas instead of to campus, the financial strain on some schools was immense. Enrollment was down across the board which meant fewer classes, fewer resources and fewer jobs for faculty, staff and administration. Some institutions saw their sustainability come into doubt. In fact, President Roosevelt intoned that the special consideration be given to colleges and universities whose existence would be in doubt in the absence of their selection.[8]

Purdue University was amongst the 1,600 schools applying for inclusion to the Navy College Training Program, although the suspense was far less palpable than it would be at other institutions. Edward C. Elliott, the president at Purdue for the last two decades, was heavily involved in the selection process. As the chief of the Division of Professional and Technical Training for the War Manpower Commission, Elliott headed up the nine-person committee for the selection of schools.[9]

Schools were selected based on a number of criteria including physical and academic structure already in place, geographic location, the presence of preexisting ROTC programs and a variety of other factors. In all, 131 institutions were selected with each designated for what type of training would be available on campus. Categories included Basic, Engineering, Marines and Pre-medical and Pre-dental.[11] Some schools were selected for only one type of training while others, like Purdue, would feature all four disciplines. Colleges and universities were chosen in 43 of the 48 states and programs ranged in size from 68 trainees at Webb Institute of Naval Architecture to nearly 2,000 trainees at Dartmouth.[11]

Once a school was selected for the program, a contract had to be drawn up between the Navy and the college and since they varied in size and service, each contract had to be unique to that institution. The Navy was responsible for room, board, instructional costs and several other financial considerations for each trainee. Another Purdue man was heavily involved in these contracts. R.B. Stewart, the controller at the university, was appointed chairman of the board for the Joint Army and Navy Board for Training Contracts.[12] Stewart helped set a baseline for what all contracts between the military and the universities must include and traveled the country to make certain all issues were resolved. A longtime advisor to the Navy on contract matters, after he got the joint task force appointment, Stewart turned down a commission from the Navy as he wanted to maintain impartiality as a civilian.[13]

After shepherding the college training program process, Stewart continued his work with the Secretary of War. A few years later, he played an integral part in the creation of the G.I. Bill, which was signed into law in 1944 and would help to fundamentally change higher education after the war. As millions of soldiers, sailors and Marines returned home after the war, the GI Bill gave many an opportunity for education that hadn't existed before. By 1947 49% of college students were there because of the G.I. Bill. Nearly 8 million WWII veterans attained some form of higher education within a decade of the war's conclusion.[14]

Stewart would continue in his role at Purdue until 1961, playing a major role in the expansion of the university. With his financial stewardship over nearly four decades, enrollment went from 3,000 to 22,000 while the campus and the university's endowment grew exponentially. He even eventually donated his house to the university to serve as the residence of the school's president.[15]

With schools selected and the financial terms between the military and the universities worked out, the only thing missing were the trainees themselves. It was determined that men already selected to the Navy's V-1, V-5 and V-7 programs would be rolled into the newly minted V-12. But those numbers were well short of what was needed. So a nationwide exam was set up in April 1943 to identify good officer candidates among current college students and high school seniors. More than 300,000 young men took the exam and those who met the minimum academic standard were passed on to an interview and physical exam.[16] In the end, 16,000 young men were selected to take part in the program as a result of the testing process, with roughly half of them reporting to their training university on July 1 and the other half on November 1.[17]

Participants who were already enrolled in colleges or universities were given special consideration on an individual basis. Upperclassmen were assigned to their current school whenever possible, as long as that school had the training designation that was needed. If, for instance a future Marine was at a school without a Marine training designation, they were transferred to a school in close proximity that did have that option. The same was true of academic considerations. If a student studying, say, mechanical engineering was assigned a school that did not offer that academic major, all efforts were made to transfer that student to a college that would offer mechanical engineering.[18]

Another decision in the administration of the program was whether to open the V-12 option up to African-America candidates. President Roosevelt issued executive order 8802 in June 1941 that ended discrimination in the armed forces but units would remain segregated until 1948.[19] Because of their recent broad inclusion to the ranks, there were no African-American officers at the outset of the war, despite there being thousands of black sailors deployed. In all, fewer than 100 African-Americans were enrolled in the V-12 program and Purdue was the only school on that list that had African-American Marine trainees.[20] One of them went on to make history.

* * * * *

In 1943, Frederick C. Branch was drafted into the Army and was later selected to become a Marine. He was enrolled at Temple University studying physics and had taken the Army's admissions test for its officer training program but was denied. Branch shipped off to Montford Point, Camp Lejeune, N.C., to the all-black boot camp used by the Marines. While there, he noticed that all of the commanding officers were white, even though their charges were black. As a response, Branch applied to Officers Training School, but was denied.

Branch was sent to the South Pacific where his detailed nature caught the eye of his commanding officer. When Branch informed the man that he had been turned down for officer's training, his superior vowed to get that application pushed through. He did just that.[21]

In 1944, Branch was admitted into the V-12 program and sent to Purdue University for his classroom training. The only African-American in his class of 250, Branch made the dean's list whilst at Purdue.[22]

Branch received his officer's commission on November 10, 1945, becoming the first black officer in the 170-year history of the United States Marines.[23] He was a first lieutenant, eventually given the command of an artillery unit stationed at Camp Pendleton, Calif. Branch eventually joined the Marine Reserves and attained the rank of captain before leaving the military in 1955 after the Korean War.[24]

Branch founded the science department at Dobbins High School in Philadelphia, putting his physics degree to good use. He taught at Dobbins until his retirement in 1988. In 1997, Branch was recognized by the Marine Corps when a building was named in his honor at Quantico, the same place he had undergone officer's training more than five decades earlier.[25] For generations to come, future officers of all races would make their way through the facility named for the man who blazed the trail for them.

*****

While on campus enrolled as V-12 trainees, the men in the program were required to meet some very strict guidelines to remain in the program. As students, they were required to take a course load of at least 17 credit hours per semester. On top of that, the men were required to participate in a minimum of nine and a half hours of physical training per week, over the course of six days. They were schooled year-round in an accelerated fashion, with three trimesters lasting four months each. And the amount of training required to complete the program was based on the amount of education and training each man entered the program with.[26]

But, busy as they were, there was still time left over for extracurricular activities. At some schools, trainees joined the campus newspaper staff or, on several occasions, started their own publications. Most universities saw Navy men make their way into the entertainment realm in the form of stage shows, orchestras and bands. At Millsaps College in Mississippi, a young man from Nebraska put on regular magic shows under the stage name of "Kit" Carson. When he was off stage, folks called him by his given name of John. After the war, he would finish his schooling and get started in a career in television with the more familiar moniker of Johnny Carson.[27] And, of course, there were fraternities, church groups, student government and a variety of other activities to pass the time.

One area that caused quite a bit of debate was whether V-12 trainees would be allowed to take part in intercollegiate athletics at their new schools. Commander Gene Tunney, the man in charge of the physical training portion of the V-12 curriculum, was opposed to allowing trainees to compete in collegiate sports. Tunney, the former heavyweight boxing champion of the world, had President Roosevelt's ear so it appeared he may win the day. However, there was stiff opposition on this point led by Admiral Randall Jacobs, the Navy's Chief of Personnel. After much deliberation, it was announced by the Secretary of the Navy that participation in intercollegiate athletics would be permitted as long as some ground rules were met. Freshmen would not be eligible to compete; the sports must not interfere with the overall mission of the V-12 program and activities could not take trainees away from campus for more than 48 hours.[28]

This decision gave thousands of trainees the opportunity to compete on campus for the next several years. For quite a few of them, it meant they could continue playing football, basketball, baseball or any variety of the sports they had taken part in at their original schools. This led to the awkward situation for some to compete against their former team, sometimes in the same season they had been a member of that original squad. No matter how you put it, having the V-12 transfers made a lot of programs stronger than they may have been previously and it provided a unifying force on campus and in towns that desperately needed to rally around something.

CHAPTER 4

CONCERNS ON CAMPUS

With the university's function for the war laid out in the academic sense, there were still plenty of questions on the athletic side in many places. While the 1941-42 winter sports seasons continued after the attack on Pearl Harbor, discussions needed to be had on how college sports would continue to be considered a vital part of the university system in the years to come.

With these questions in mind, athletics directors from the Big Ten Conference met in early March 1942 in Chicago's Windermere Hotel to talk through the issues of the day. Among the items discussed was the possible suspension of the prohibition on freshmen eligibility for the coming year. This was a nation-wide issue seen by many as a necessary measure given that every campus was losing droves of male students, and male student-athletes, to the military. Other issues at hand were the necessity of schedule flexibility, the inclusion of competition against military installations, and the adjustment of eligibility requirements.[1]

All of these issues were really just symptoms of the larger problem on the horizon for college athletics directors. A spokesman for the conference laid it out in a statement with a representative from the United Press syndicate.

"If the war is a long one and the occasion ever arises when there is a cry to abolish all athletic competition, we want to be able to go before the government officials and show that wartime sports have their place in the national scheme," the anonymous conference representative said.[2]

Midwestern military installations such as Great Lakes Naval Station near Chicago, Camp Grant in Rockford, Illinois, and Iowa Pre-Flight in Iowa City would be fielding athletic teams in the coming years and would need competitors. It was incumbent on Big Ten institutions to provide just that in order to strengthen their own relevancy in the eyes of national leaders.

The athletics director for Great Lakes Naval Station, Lt. Comm. J. Russell Cook spoke to the assembled group on this subject.[3] He was the only military leader in attendance but not the only outsider in the room. Representatives from the University of Pittsburgh and Notre Dame were also in attendance. Pittsburgh had actually been positioning itself to join the league if the University of Chicago were to drop out so it was in their interests to be involved whenever possible. Notre Dame football coach Frank Leahy was there, meanwhile, because of close geographical ties and the fact that he had four games with Big Ten schools on the Irish's schedule in 1942.[4]

As the leaders gathered to address their problems and prove their vitality in Chicago, they couldn't hold back the tide. The fall of 1942 saw many college campuses missing ever-larger numbers of male students as enlistment approached 4 million by the end of the year. In what was a sign of things to come, 60 colleges canceled their football seasons for the fall of 1942.[5] But the sport itself powered forward.

On the field, Ohio State, Georgia and Wisconsin all laid claim to a piece of the national championship. The military installations had things rolling as well as more than half of the 22 service teams across the country posted winning records.[6] As for the Boilermakers, well, they weren't so fortunate.

The season began to come apart in February of 1942 when head coach and athletics director Allen Henry "Mal" Elward decided to leave the university to rejoin the U.S. Navy. Elward had first enlisted during WWI, attaining the rank of lieutenant, senior grade. In a letter to President Elliott and the Board of Trustees, Elward was very succinct:

> To the President and Trustees of Purdue University:
>
> I greatly appreciate your recent offer to extend my contract as head football coach from June 30 to December 31, 1942.
> However, after due and careful consideration of the matter, I have come to the conclusion that I can better serve my country in these perilous times in some other position.
> Therefore, I have already made application to re-join the Navy and hereby tender my resignation as coach.
>
> Respectfully submitted,
> MAL ELWARD[7]

The process to replace Elward was swift and decisive. Within a week of accepting the former coach's resignation, the President and Trustees promoted from within, hiring Elmer Burnham to be the leader on the gridiron.[8] Burnham had been on Elward's staff since the 1935, serving as the freshman coach.

At the same time, the university leaders had to fill the post of Athletic Director. For this, they looked, once again, to the football coaching staff. Former Purdue offensive lineman and current assistant varsity coach Guy "Red" Mackey was elevated to head the department. Mackey, just 37 years old at the time, was thrilled to be entrusted with the future of the school that he had grown to love. In a statement following his hiring, Mackey said, "I am delighted to have the opportunity to serve my alma mater in this new capacity. Purdue has grown to be a part of my life and I hope that I am able to justify the confidence that has been placed in me." [8]

Mackey did indeed justify the confidence of President Elliott and the trustees, serving as head of the athletics department for some 29 years before retiring in 1971, while helping to usher the department into the modern era of college athletics.

Still, even with the leaders of the team and the athletics department, the 1942 season was a struggle for the Boilermakers. The team finished with a record of 1-8 with that lone win coming against a Northwestern team that also finished with a single victory in 1942. The Boilermakers were held scoreless five times and scored just 27 points in the entire season. Purdue was the only team in the conference to not have a single player earn either first-team or second-team All-Big Ten honors. It was the worst Purdue season in two decades and amongst the worst in program history.[10]

By the spring of 1943, the forecast hadn't brightened. The toll of the war on the university was becoming ever greater as men of a certain age continued to enlist and head overseas. The issue was brought up that it might be best for the university to put the football program on hold for the duration of the war, a discussion that was being had at schools across the country. More than 100 colleges and universities across the country had already made the decision to cancel football for the fall of 1943. Most of the schools in the Southeastern Conference, including Alabama, Auburn, Florida and Tennessee canceled their seasons. The Pacific Coast Conference was hit hard as well with Stanford, Oregon, Oregon State and Washington State pulling out. Other prominent programs that made the hard decision included Boston College, Fordham and Harvard. Manpower and monetary considerations were the main reasons for these decisions.[11]

The college game wasn't alone as the National Football League also had to take drastic measures to have a season in the fall of 1943. The Cleveland Rams suspended operations after having several players and majority owner Dan Reeves drafted.[12] Meanwhile, The Pittsburgh Steelers and the Philadelphia Eagles merged to become the "Steagles" for the 1943 season.[13]

Merging programs wasn't an option on the college level but the shortage of men was still a very real problem. Ohio State University's head coach Paul Brown was facing a seemingly impossible situation. His 1942 squad had prospered finishing 9-1 and winning the national championship on the strength of a team that featured five All-Americans. By the spring of 1943, his squad was decimated by the various military service call-ups. Of the 37 returning members for the Buckeyes, 30 ended up heading off to fight for their nation.[14] Fellow Big Ten Coach Ray Eliot of the University of Illinois actually canceled spring drills when the Army called 43 of his 51 players to active duty.[15]

The University of Iowa, meanwhile, had its own version of that same problem. The Hawkeyes lost their entire coaching staff to active duty in the spring of 1943, including head coach Eddie Anderson who took a leave of absence to join the U.S. Army Medical Corps.[16]

Under these conditions, coach Burnham opened his team's spring practice season inside Lambert Fieldhouse. Burnham's squad of 45 men had to share the indoor facility with the Track & Field team and the baseball team, both of which were now in season.[17] Burnham spent his practice time working on the fundamentals, as most coaches do with inexperienced teams. However, it was even more important in this situation to focus on learning the basics, as many of the mainstays from the 1942 season did not return for spring drills. In fact, Burnham faced the challenge of getting enough men together for his spring practices to the point that he resorted to unconventional recruiting measures in trying to get male students to come out for football. Burnham began appealing to the patriotic nature of the students, urging them to consider coming out as a means for keeping themselves in shape in case their country called them to service.[18]

To make matters worse, the challenge of diminished numbers was met with an influx of players of diminutive size. But, while the veterans were few and far between, they did exist on the spring squad. Guard Dick Barwegen was returning after a very good junior season. Junior tackle Gene Matrewitz also reported for spring ball, giving the Boilermakers a fair amount of experience on the front line. In the backfield, Henry Stram was returning after a solid performance in his sophomore season.[19]

Although Barwegen would go on to star on the 1943 team, Matrewitz and Stram left the university for active service before the beginning of the fall term.[20] Stram would return in 1946 and finish his Purdue career, playing two more years, before eventually getting into coaching and leading the Kansas City Chiefs to a victory in Super Bowl IV. This, of course, all came after he became known by the moniker Hank Stram. But in the spring of 1943, 'Hurrying Henry' Stram was one of the great hopes for the Boilermaker squad.

So, Burnham and his coaching staff spent the spring instructing a group of Purdue students who had little experience to try and prepare them for a season he wasn't sure was going to happen. In an effort to drum up interest and perhaps add a few bodies to the roster, Burnham issued a call to student body, looking for anyone interested in joining the football team. In a May 20, 1943, article, the student newspaper laid out the desperate measure. "Burnham has stated that if any student is interested in participating in varsity football next fall and believes they will still be in school at that time, he should contact Coach Burnham sometime this week." [21]

A few weeks earlier, Burnham and Mackey headed back to Chicago for the annual Big Ten meetings. At these meetings, officials from universities around the nation were told by Army and Navy representatives that the fate of the seasons would be left up to each individual school while once again encouraging the schools to schedule as many games as possible with the various military institutions that had popped up because of the war. Schools were also encouraged to replace games that were too far away with games with more locally-based military installations. This directly affected Purdue's scheduled game in New York City against powerful Fordham University. The Boilermakers' fall slate would take another hit as a non-conference battle with Michigan State was scrapped when the Spartans decided they would not play in the fall.[22]

By mid-May 1943, the outlook at changed significantly on campus. Purdue was selected host both the Army Specialized Training Program and the Navy College Training Program.[23] In a matter of weeks, the university would be welcoming nearly a thousand soldiers, 800 sailors and 450 Marines to campus. With an additional 2,200 men headed to campus, being able to field a football team was no longer in question. What kind of team this transient group would be able to make up was another question altogether. Fortunately for the Boilermakers, the men at the helm were perfectly matched to the challenges ahead.

CHAPTER 5

THE MEN WHO WOULD LEAD THEM

Like with many football programs in the first half of the 20th-century, particularly in the Midwest, the influence of mighty Notre Dame was quite pronounced at Purdue. More specifically, the influence of the great Knute Rockne could be felt for decades in West Lafayette. It started with James Phelan, the first great coach for the Boilermakers, who played quarterback for the Fighting Irish from 1915 to 1917 while Rockne was in his early days as an assistant coach. His playing career was cut short midway through his senior year when Phelan, the captain of the Irish, was drafted into the Army as the nation geared up for entry into World War I.[1]

Upon returning to civilian life, Phelan entered coaching, heading up the program at the University of Missouri. Phelan led the Tigers to a 13-3 record in two seasons before heading back to Indiana in time for the 1922 season, taking charge of the Boilermakers.[2] In eight seasons with Purdue, Phelan led the Boilermakers to a 35-22-5 record, including an undefeated 1929 season in which the program won its first outright Big Ten title and finished ranked #2 in the country.[3]

Phelan's top assistant and eventual successor was a fellow whose greatest attributes perfectly matched his name. Noble Kizer took over the Purdue program in 1930 after Phelan, the Portland, Ore. native, returned to the Pacific Northwest to coach the University of Washington.[4] Kizer also played for Rockne at Notre Dame, as a guard for Irish in the 1920s, paving the way for the famed "Four Horsemen" and winning a national title along the way.[5]

As the head man at Purdue, Kizer continued to build on Phelan's success before having to step away from coaching for health reasons following the 1936 season.[6] Kizer compiled a phenomenal 42-13-3 record in his seven years at the helm, including winning two Big Ten titles and a share of the 1931 National title with Pittsburgh and USC.[7] Even after stepping away as head coach, Kizer continued in his role as athletics director, a position he had held since 1933.

Mal Elward stepped in to lead the football program following Kizer's abrupt exit from the team. A bit older that his two predecessors on the sidelines, Elward still had connections to Rockne. The two were teammates for two years at Notre Dame.[8] Elward was brought to Purdue by Phelan to be an assistant ahead of the 1927 season. The Boilermakers were a bit more up and down under Elward, winning only about half the time.[9] And when Elward decided to leave the university in early 1942 to return to the Navy, the next man up was Elmer Burnham. And though Burnham ended up in the same place as the men proceeding him, his path was significantly less conventional.

Elmer Burnham was hired by Kizer in 1935 and came to Purdue to serve as the coach of the Boilermakers' freshmen team.[10] Burnham arrived from South Bend Central High School, where he'd been an integral part of the athletics program for nearly 20 years.[11] Originally from New England, Burnham attended Springfield YMCA College in Springfield, Mass., which had gained some notoriety as the birthplace of the game of basketball, the brainchild of graduate student James Naismith, in 1891.

Burnham starred in four sports for the Chiefs, playing football, basketball, baseball and tennis.[12] Burnham actually didn't play football until he arrived a Springfield as his hometown high school in West Newbury, Massachusetts, was not large enough to field a team.[13] But once he arrived on campus, he took to the sport immediately.

After two years at Springfield, he took a job from as the assistant director of the South Bend YMCA and headed west to Indiana. It was recommended by his superiors in Springfield that taking a year of job training would be a good idea since Burnham's youthful looks might make it difficult for him to get a job after graduation.[14] It was during this time in South Bend that Burnham made connections that would eventually land him back in northwest Indiana following graduation. In the summer of 1916, he was hired by South Bend High School (later South Bend Central) to coach football, basketball and baseball, before eventually adding athletics director to his title.[14]

Burnham's first football squad in the fall of 1916 went undefeated but his coaching career would soon be put on hold. With the country's entry into World War I, Burnham enlisted in the Army. He served in a Trench Mortar Battery, attaining the rank of sergeant before his honorable discharge in 1919.[15] Burnham returned to South Bend Central and coached there for the next 14 years, quickly turning the Bears into a dominant force. Burnham's teams compiled a record of 118-30-8 on the gridiron, winning three conference crowns and a state championship.[16]

But Burnham wasn't content with just having success on the high school gridiron. Over the course of his tenure in South Bend, he continued to better himself in the classroom by taking coursework at Notre Dame.[17] Springfield YMCA College was a three-year program at the time so he worked on his remaining credits toward a Bachelor of Science degree, which he received in the spring of 1935.[18] Burnham also attended several coaching clinics run by none other than Knute Rockne, a man he had befriended from his early days in South Bend during various YMCA events.[19]

Burnham's on-field success, along with the relationships he'd built in nearly two decades in Indiana, made him an easy choice for Purdue University when Noble Kizer was looking for a mentor for the freshmen team. After all, though he wasn't exactly a direct descendant from the Rockne Tree, he was about as close as you could get to it.

When it was announced Burnham was leaving South Bend Central High School, a banquet was held in his honor. More than 400 friends, fans and fellow coaches attended to honor the man who had done so much for the community. Among those in attendance was a bright, young English teacher who had recently graduated from the institution Burnham was headed to. The young man would take over the baseball program from Burnham and was to be an assistant with the basketball team. John Wooden would coach at South Bend Central for nine years before joining the Navy and, of course, going on to great acclaim as the perhaps most celebrated, and most decorated, college basketball coach ever.[20]

Burnham would serve as the freshmen coach for the Boilermakers while Kizer and Elward led the varsity. But his temperament and knowledge made Burnham a very popular figure amongst the team. Kizer once referred to Burnham as "the most outstanding high school coach in the Midwest, capable of handling any college varsity job that I know of."[21] So, when Elward announced he was re-enlisting in the Navy, Burnham was the natural choice to succeed him. He had the full support of the team and, it turned out, the full support of the Purdue Board of Trustees who approved Burnham as head coach and Guy "Red" Mackey as athletics director by unanimous votes.[22] Following his appointment by the board, Burnham spoke of what the job meant to him.

"I feel deeply honored to be entrusted with the football coaching responsibilities," he said. "Purdue has a long tradition for fighting football teams. In order to uphold that tradition, I know it will require the fullest cooperation of the players, students and all other friends of Purdue Football. Knowing Purdue Spirit as I do, I sincerely hope that we'll be able to accomplish our purpose."[23]

Burnham took over the Purdue football program on March 1, 1942. And while the 1942 squad endured a forgettable year, going 1-8 while being shut out five times, the important thing was the team persevered though there were just 41 men on the roster.[24]

In the spring of 1943, as the team was holding offseason practice, the reality of the world continued to hit the Boilermakers. Just 45 men showed for the first day of practice and, as Coach Burnham later put it, "We have a lot of 135 pounds on our squad."[25] Saying the men were undersized was an understatement. Burnham also estimated some 60-percent of the freshman squad from the previous fall had not returned to campus for one reason or another.[26] Of course, the most common reason was plain as day: most had volunteered for or been drafted to the war effort.

Promising halfback Henry Stram was drafted into the U.S. Army in late April and would be leaving the team in the weeks to come despite having taken part in the spring drills.[27] "Hurrying Henry" would serve in the Army Air Corps until the end of the war before returning to Purdue to conclude his playing career and complete his degree in 1946-

47. Stram would go on to coach the Purdue Baseball team for nearly a decade before heading to greener pastures, eventually leading the Kansas City Chiefs to a Super Bowl title in a Hall of Fame career.[28]

Assistant football coach, and head baseball man, William "Dutch" Fehring also received orders to report to Navy pre-flight training school in late April.[29] Burnham's club ended its spring sessions with as much uncertainty as ever. By the end of summer, the ranks of assistant coaches had been thinned yet again. Freshmen coach Emmett Lowery, who also worked with the ends on the varsity squad, was activated by the Navy.[30] Lowery had played football and basketball with the Boilermakers a decade earlier and was in his second season coaching with his alma mater when he was called up. Backfield coach Mel Taube was also on leave after being activated by the U.S. Naval Reserves.[31]

That left Burnham with just two assistants from the previous year: Claude Reeck and Sam Voinoff. Reeck was an able assistant but his football coaching was a secondary concern at Purdue. Reeck was the head wrestling coach for the Boilermakers and a darn good one. He led the Boilermakers to five Big Ten titles in his three decades in charge of the Purdue grapplers.[32] Voinoff, meanwhile, had starred on two Big Ten championship football teams with the Boilermakers from 1929-31.[33] He coached at his alma mater from 1937-50 at which time he embarked on a second career…as the head coach of the Purdue Golf program, where he led the Boilermakers to 10 Big Ten titles and one NCAA Championship on the links.[34] But in the fall of 1943, he would mentor the men on the front lines for Burnham.

The Boilermakers had a few vacancies to fill in the summer of 1943. One of those spots was taken care of as a great candidate fell into their laps. Saint Joseph's College, just up the road from West Lafayette in Rensselaer, Ind., had announced they were canceling football for the 1943 season, despite coming off of back-to-back undefeated seasons.[35] That meant the man who had led St. Joe's to such heights was now available. That man happened to be a Lafayette-native by the name of Joe Dienhart. Dienhart had played briefly at Notre Dame before closing his college career out at Butler University.[36] He then became a successful high school coach in Indianapolis before taking the job with Saint Joseph's. With the 1943 season on the horizon, Dienhart needed a job and Burnham needed another assistant coach to fill out his staff.

The other opening required a lot more work of Mackey and

Burnham as they decided to take a big swing in attempting to convince the premier quarterback in the National Football League to walk away from the game in his prime. In the end, Cecil Isbell did just that.

Isbell had a great career with the Boilermakers in the mid-30s, earning team MVP honors in 1937.[37] He was taken with the seventh-overall pick in the 1938 NFL Draft by the Green Bay Packers.[38] Early in his pro career, Isbell split time at quarterback with Arnie Herber, eventually beating out the future Pro Football Hall of Famer for the starting job.[39] Isbell was quick on his feet and a very good passer and he led the Packers in rushing and passing his rookie year. Playing for the legendary Curly Lambeau, Isbell and the Packers won the World Championship in his second season and he had supplanted Herber as the starter by 1940, allowing Green Bay to let Herber go to the New York Giants.[40]

Isbell was the best quarterback in the NFL in 1941 and 1942 as he perfected Lambeau's "Notre Dame Box" offense and forged a great connection with Don Hutson, one of the best receivers in the history of the game.[41] In 1941, Isbell set an NFL record with 1,479 passing yards and in 1942, he broke it while becoming the first quarterback to ever surpass 2,000 yards in a season through the air.[42] In the process, Hutson set records in virtually every receiving category, some of which stood for decades.

Isbell and Hutson had actually come to West Lafayette in the spring of 1942 to serve as instructors for the annual Purdue Coaches Clinic.[43] It would lay the groundwork for what was to transpire a little over a year later. In the fall of 1942, Isbell had the greatest season a quarterback had ever experience in the NFL, setting single-season records for passing yards, completions, touchdowns and completion percentage.[44] He also threw a touchdown in 23 consecutive games from 1940-42, his final 23 games in Green Bay.[45]

When Lambeau caught wind of Purdue's plan to steal his signal caller, the man who founded the Packers decades earlier did all he could to keep his star pupil. Lambeau offered Isbell the title of backfield coach in addition to being the starting quarterback. Isbell turned it down, along with his $10,000 a year salary, and retired from the NFL just a few days past his 28th birthday to head back to West Lafayette.[46] At the time, Isbell said the Packers' penchant for releasing aging players played into his decision.

"I saw Lambeau go around the locker room and tell players like

Arnie Herber they were done," Isbell said. "I vowed that would never happen to me."[47]

When asked a few years later to name the greatest passer ever, Lambeau did not equivocate. "Isbell was a master at any range – short, medium or long," Lambeau said. "He could throw soft passes, bullet ones or feathery lobs. He's the best with Sid Luckman of the Bears a close second and Sammy Baugh a long third."[48]

Isbell would be the backfield coach, in charge of installing the passing game that he had set the NFL on fire with and calling the bulk of the plays. Purdue fans were thrilled with the development on several different levels. It was great to be able to talk the premier offensive talent in the pros to come take charge of the Boilermaker attack. And it was a great sign for the prestige of the program that Isbell would walk away from one of the highest salaries in the NFL to come coach the team. But the cherry on top was that Isbell was one of their own…a Boilermaker who had taken the NFL by storm and would now hope to do the same thing for his alma mater.

Burnham's coaching staff was finally in place. The real question that remained was who were the men that they'd be leading?

CHAPTER 6

THE BOYS ON THE TEAM

The Navy men arrived on campus on July 5 to begin the V-12 program. They spent the first week getting registered, fitted for uniforms, measured, tested and acclimated to their new lives. Then the routine began with classes, calisthenics and a strict schedule. Each day began with reveille at 5:45 a.m. followed by exercise form 6-6:20 a.m., breakfast at 6:45a.m. and classes at 8. The trainees lived in Cary Hall and various fraternity houses given over to the Navy. They dined at Cary and the Union as the fraternity house kitchens were closed for the summer. There was a 10 p.m. curfew each night and lights out at midnight. This would be their lives for the next 16 weeks.[1]

Because of the nature of the 1943 season and the shifting of personnel from school to school, to say nothing of the shifting of men to active duty, the NCAA made an important ruling in late spring. They would allow schools to hold summer training camps.[2]

For Burnham's boys, the camp began on July 15th in West Lafayette and would last four weeks. A few days prior, Burnham met with Commander Hugh J. Bartley, the commanding officer of the Naval Training Station at Purdue. The two men discussed their two programs and worked out a way for both to exist together, as the V-12 program had a strict regimen that it required its trainees to follow for obvious reasons. And there would be no questioning which program had priority.[3]

Burnham called a meeting for the evening of July 14th, the night before camp was to begin. It was his first official chance to see what would comprise the 1943 team.[4] He knew that running back Ed Cycenas was the only letter-winner he had returning from the 1942 team. Cycenas had started in the backfield the previous year and was actually a member of the V-12 program himself. He just had the good fortune of being assigned to his current school when orders came down. Burnham knew that there were a fair number of V-12 transfers coming in who had played at their previous schools. But their taking part in football was certainly not a given considering the demands they were facing due to their Navy obligations. Burnham hoped for a good turnout.

He got that and more. In all, 93 men turned out for the meeting. Burnham set the tone for the year in addressing the group.

"We ought to have a lot of fun," he said. "You have shown by your attendance at tonight's meeting that you enjoy football and we hope to give you a chance at that kind of competition you like. One thing is certain, regardless of where you may have come from, you won't meet any stiffer opposition than is provided by our schedule this fall."[5]

Burnham also informed the men that he had discussed their involvement with Commander Bartley and that the Navy's official position was one of encouragement for their taking part in football, provided it didn't conflict with their service responsibilities.[6] The players would also have their classroom work constantly scrutinized to make sure they weren't falling behind in that area as their education was a critical part of their Naval training.

Burnham laid out a practice schedule that would see the team work out from 4:10 to 5:30 each afternoon for the next four weeks. The first three weeks of the summer session would focus on fundamentals, conditioning and basic skill work while the final week would be full contact and scrimmaging.[7]

V-12 members made up a vast majority of the initial group. There were 23 Navy men and 46 Marines and fewer than two dozen civilians amongst the group. It also included 30 players who had earned varsity letters at their former schools.[8] And although there may have been some initial concern that the new transfers might have a little too much going on in their lives to concentrate on football, that doesn't appear to be the case from contemporary practice reports.

The team was noted to have a great enthusiasm at the daily practices, each man eager to prove themselves to a coaching staff that was trying to figure out what it had on the fly. Perhaps it was the way their immersion into a child's game contrasted with the stark reality they faced in every other aspect of their live outside of the practice field. Or maybe it was Burnham's challenge that the focus of the season, first and foremost, was to have a good time. Whatever the reason, despite hot July temperatures and the normally mundane tasks of fundamental drills, the players hustled from one station to the next, thoroughly enjoying themselves.[9]

By the third day of practice, the number of participants had grown to 101 men on the practice field. By the end of the second week, it had ballooned to 134.[10] Longtime athletics public relations man Bob Woodworth was good-naturedly joking with Burnham at practice during that second week claiming Great Lakes Naval Station, Purdue's season-opening opponent, needed to get a starting lineup so they could work on their game program. Burnham laughed, turned to Woodworth and told the PR man to go ahead and select his own lineup.[11]

One thing the coaching staff was clear about was a desire to build a team rather than a group of individuals. About two weeks into the summer session, Burnham spoke of this need, not just as a philosophical approach but as a pragmatic one.

"My team will be built as a team and not as a team of individuals," Burnham said. "Because of the draft and the uncertainty of the status of any of the players who are in the armed services, it would be very unwise to build a squad around one particular star. Any coach doing so would be left holding the bag if that one player was transferred or changed to another location."[12]

The coaching staff was doing its best to get a fair appraisal of the talent at hand while playing things fairly close to the vest. They made a habit of dividing the squad into different groups one day and then completely changing things for the following day's practice. This allowed the coaches to see the men working in different situations and with different teammates while not giving anything away as to who may have a leg up. It didn't help matters that the NCAA mandated that the first three weeks be fundamentals only with no contact or scrimmaging allowed.[13]

By the end of the third week, the calendar having turned to August and the oppressive heat having settled in for the duration, Burnham dressed his entire team in full pads and helmets for the first time. The first full-contact practice was still a few days off but he wanted to get the team used to playing in the full uniform once again.[14]

As camp continued, it became apparent to the coaches that the offense should favor the T-formation. This offense featured seven men across the offensive line, a quarterback under center and three men abreast in the backfield, a fullback flanked on either side by halfbacks. It was one of the oldest football strategies in existence, having been popular as early as the 1880s, with Walter Camp getting credit from many for its creation. It went out of vogue with the creation of the forward pass but had a resurgence in the early 1940s, with several NFL teams and a few prominent colleges featuring the formation.

From a personnel standpoint, this formation made a lot of sense for Burnham's boys as the roster featured a formidable offensive front and plenty of experience in the backfield. And the "T" had the benefit of being both very simple and incredibly versatile. The base set of plays included basic handoffs to each of the three backs on inside or outside runs. But as the players became more comfortable with the timing and the complexities of the formation, fake handoffs and misdirection, counter-action runs and play-action passes made the options nearly limitless. It also helped that the two men vying for the starting position at quarterback had both run the T-formation at their previous schools.

Sam Vacanti had run the T while calling signals the previous year at Iowa for future Hall of Fame coach Eddie Anderson. Vacanti, a Marine trainee from Omaha, Neb., had been a reserve for the 1942 Hawkeyes, helping the squad to a winning record including an upset of second-ranked Wisconsin.[15] His counterpart, James "Junior" Darr ran the T-formation for another Hall of Fame coach, Don Faurot with the Missouri Tigers. Darr was also a Marine and had helped Mizzou to a conference title the year before. He was actually one of seven players on the squad who had earned varsity letters for the Tigers in

1942.[16]

And while Missouri was well represented, it couldn't hold a candle to the University of Illinois. Twelve Boilermakers had played previously for the conference rival located just 90 miles from West Lafayette. The best among the former Illini players, and perhaps the best on the team, was a junior guard named Alex Agase. Standing just 5'10" and weighing less than 200 pounds, Agase played like a giant, earning All-America honors for the Fighting Illini the previous season.[17] Agase was joined on the line by fellow Marine trainees and former Illini players John Genis and Mike Kasap. All three men had earned all-conference honors in the 1942 season. And all three men hailed from the Land of Lincoln and elected to attend their state school before the war broke out.[18]

Fullback Tony Butkovich had a lot in common with his fellow former Fighting Illini teammates. He was also training to be a Marine. He had also earned varsity letters at Illinois in both 1941 and 1942.[19] And he also hailed from the state of Illinois. A native of the village of St. David, Butkovich starred at nearby Lewiston High School in the late 1930s. In fact, it wasn't just football that Butkovich starred in at Lewiston. He was also a standout guard on the basketball team and a baseball player widely regarded to have major league potential.[20] He was looking forward to playing along-side his little brother Bill in 1943 with the Illini but the V-12 program had other ideas, shipping the elder Butkovich to Purdue.

Although he was a star in high school, it hadn't quite translated to the college game yet for Butkovich. Playing halfback as a sophomore in 1941, Butkovich had found playing time but couldn't crack the starting lineup for the 2-6 Illinois squad.[21] As a junior in 1942, it was more of the same. Illinois was better under first-year head coach Ray Eliot but Butkovich split time in the backfield with senior Jimmy Smith. Smith was a captain for the Fighting Illini and one of the real emotional leaders on the team. But he was also quite small for a man playing such a vital role, listed on the roster as around 170 pounds and widely regarded as the smallest fullback in the conference.[22] In fact, the size disparity between the two men came into play during the signature win of the 1942 season for the Illini.

Facing off against two-time defending national champion Minnesota early in the year and trying to break the Gophers' 18-game winning streak against other college opponents, the Illini knew they were undermanned. His team trailing 7-6 at halftime, Coach Eliot pulled his two fullbacks aside.

Looking at Smith, Eliot said, "Tony, you'll probably play most of this half. I think we need all the beef we can use."

Without missing a beat, Smith replied, "Don't hesitate Ray. Do whatever you have to do to win this game!"[23]

That faith was rewarded late in the third quarter after Minnesota scored to tie the game at 13. Butkovich burst through the line on the PAT attempt and blocked the kick. Interestingly, it was Butkovich's best friend and future fellow Purdue Marine Alex Agase the was the hero on the day. Agase recovered not one but two fumbles for touchdowns from his defensive line position, including the game winner in late in the fourth quarter as the Fighting Illini pulled it out 20-13. After the game, the team decided Agase could attain whatever elected office he decided to seek. Meanwhile, Butkovich waited as long as he could to change out of his uniform, simply not wanting the moment to end.

"I never want to get dressed," Butkovich said to Coach Eliot when he was told he'd better get out of his wet uniform. "I never want to leave. Who said those babies were tough?"[24]

Illini climbed to No. 5 in the national polls the following week but hit a buzz saw of a schedule, with three losses in a four-week span to teams that would all finish in the nation's top ten, including eventual national champion Ohio State.[25] There were certainly moments of glory for the 1942 Illinois squad and a lot of hope for the coming season. Of course, the Navy's V-12 program intervened.

The Fighting Illini were the program best represented by the V-12 transfers on the Boilermaker squad but they were far from the only one. North Dakota, Cincinnati, Tulane, Oregon State and Iowa all were represented on the final roster with a majority of the V-12 transfers being on hand as Marine trainees.[26] But it wasn't just colleges around the country that were represented. There was also an NFL veteran on the roster.

Starting center Lou DeFilippo was a stalwart for the Fordham Rams in the late 1930s and early 1940s, leading the team to the Cotton Bowl as a senior in 1940. DeFilippo was named the team MVP of the bowl game and was drafted by the New York Giants in the sixth-round of the 1941 NFL Draft. He played for the Giants in the fall of 1941, backing up Pro Bowl center Mel Hein. By the spring of 1943, DeFilippo had signed up for the Navy officer's training program and, as a part of the V-12 program, became eligible for another season of college ball.[27] This was actually not that uncommon for the 1943 season as the Boilermakers would face off with plenty of professionals in the coming weeks.

By the time the scrimmages rolled around, the Boilermakers were ready for full contact. Three weeks of practicing in shorts had been quite enough and, as they donned their pads, the players were ready for action. The heat continued to pound down on the team in typical early-August fashion in the Midwest. But that didn't dampen the mood on the practice field.

"This is really fun," said DeFilippo to *Lafayette Journal & Courier* sports editor Gordon Graham in the midst of the scrimmage.[28] Lou the Giant and his teammates were in the midst of their first full contact work of the season on a practice field that could be best compared to a blast furnace and they couldn't have been happier. At the end of the session, even with the bumps and bruises, the blood and sweat and dust, there was an overwhelming sense of joy.[29]

"For a while there, I thought I was dying," said an unidentified Boilermaker. "Now I feel alright. A workout like that in this type of weather is good for you...gets you in shape."[30]

And while the lineup was certainly still in question, the cream had already begun to rise to the top. Putting together a starting roster had been a bit of a punchline a few weeks earlier but Burnham starting to get a handle on things: Joe Buscemi and Frank Bauman playing end, Mike Kasap and John Genis at tackle, James Laughter and James McMillian at guard and Lou DiFilippo in the middle. Sam Vacanti ran the first-team offense at quarterback with halfback Ed Cycenas and Arthur Flint at halfback and Tony Butkovich at fullback.[31]

In all, that was five former Illini players in the starting 11 to go with two Iowa Hawkeyes, two original Boilermakers, one Fordham Ram and one college football rookie. Ed Cycenas was the only Purdue letter-winner from the 1942 team in the initial two-deep. Fittingly, he was the man who scored the day's first touchdown, scampering around the right end for a 15-yard score early on in the day's action.[32]

As the scrimmages continued in the last week of summer practice sessions, the running game began to really emerge as a potent threat. Having three powerful backfield options in addition to a mobile quarterback, to go with all of the variations possible out of the T-Formation starting to show a lot of promise. And the lynchpin to it all was Butkovich.

By the third day of full contact, the brawny fullback had distinguished himself with a very diverse skill set, able to act as a battering ram through the line but agile enough to go the distance from anywhere on the field. He might run a defender over or simply scurry around a would-be tackler for a long gain. At one point during a drill, Butkovich reeled off a 60-yard run, catching the attention of everyone at the practice that day. Fellow fullback Leo Milla, a Missouri transfer, was also getting good work in and the foundation of the Boilermaker offense was emerging.[33]

Burnham continued to learn the personnel by constantly changing the roster around. If a particular offensive group had a good showing, he and his coaching staff would take note and then change things around the next day to try and bolster the defense. Two-way players were the norm for the time so splitting up the first-teamers would give a better approximation of the talent on hand. The offensive backfield would certainly be better with one of the best offensive lines in America leading the way, but what would Butkovich, Vacanti and the rest look like if Agase, Kasap and DeFilippo were on the defensive front? These are the types of questions Burnham had to wrestle with in those game-like situations.

As the Boilermakers neared the conclusion of their four-week summer camp, word had leaked out that there was something special going on in West Lafayette. Supporters had begun to show up to practice sessions early on and the number grew as the weeks unfolded. Students and community members would show up in the summer sun to take in the action. Commander H.J. Bartley, the head of the V-12 program at the university, was in attendance on most days. A big fan of football, he also had a vested interest in seeing and getting to know the men in his command. Bartley and Burnham had struck up a friendship early on as they both recognized their roles at the university were decidedly intertwined.[34]

Bartley was joined at the final day of practice by university president Edward C. Elliott, athletics director Guy "Red" Mackey and the mayor of Lafayette, Dr. Austin Killian. Mackey, the former football player and coach with the Boilermakers, spent most of the session explaining in great detail what was going on during the session, loving every moment of it.[35]

By the time the final scrimmage had rolled around on August 11th, a total of 161 men had come out at some point to try their hand at Purdue football. For some it was a curiosity that would not last much beyond the summer camp. For others, it was a way to pass the time between classes, drilling and their other duties as future military officers. But for the group of men who would go on to compete for the Boilermakers, it was the beginning of something special. And as the team prepared to break summer camp, Burnham's methods had paid off as the roster began to take shape.[36]

The men were split into two groups, the "A" squad and the "B" squad of between 50 and 60 players each. Burnham made clear that while the "A" squad would play the varsity schedule, he and his staff would do their best to put together a slate of games for the "B" squad to compete in. He also pointed out that there would be no hard line between the two groups with players able to transfer back and forth between the lineups as needed.[37]

The offensive line looked fairly well set and quite formidable. DeFilippo would start at center, backed up by a trio of fellow V-12 trainees: William Newell, Walter Poremba and Joseph Morrow. Newell had earned playing time for the Boilermakers in 1942 while Morrow transferred in from Missouri and Poremba had played freshmen ball in 1942 at Case Institute in Cleveland. Agase was an easy choice at one guard spot, having been named an All-American the previous year. The competition for the second spot was fairly open with no fewer than 15 candidates in the mix to flank the other side of the line. The list included letter-winners from Missouri, Ball State, North Dakota and Purdue. It was the Purdue man who had the inside position, however, as junior Dick Barwegen was emerging as a solid player.[38]

Genis and Kasap led a very deep and very talented group of tackles. The two Illinois transfers would be backed up by several men who had seen the field in 1942 including John Staak from the University of Iowa and Tom Hughes from Missouri, as well as men from Ohio University, Oregon State and Cincinnati. A pair of Illinois transfers led the way at end, as Joe Buscemi and Frank Bauman continued to set themselves apart from the pack, as the front line looked to have a lot of experience, even if it was from a diverse background.[39]

Heading up the backfield was the former Iowa Hawkeye, Sam Vacanti. Vacanti played halfback at Iowa but was shifted to quarterback for the Boilers to compete with Missouri transfers Jimmy Darr and Ed Gerker. Halfback was a position of largely unproven commodities, although the group was led by Ed Cycenas, the only returning major letter winner for the Old Gold and Black. He was joined in the backfield by a host of transfer students from all over, including Shurtleff College's Stanley Dubicki and Keith Parker of Missouri. And as thin as the squad was at halfback, the Boilermakers were strong at the fullback post. Four players had earned letters at their previous schools in 1942, led by Butkovich from Illinois, Bernie Tetek from Tulane, and Leo Milla and Michael Popovich from Missouri.[40]

And while Burnham was happy with the progress his team had made during the summer training sessions and optimistic about the season to come, he was still cautious.

"The enthusiasm of this squad sets a new high," Burnham said following the final summer scrimmage. "But it will take actual competition to prove its worth as a team."[41]

CHAPTER 7

| WEEK 1 |
AT GREAT LAKES

As the dawn of a new season began in West Lafayette, Ind., the same could not be said in hundreds of other college towns across the nation. Leading up to the fall of 1943, schools across the country had to weigh the possibility of canceling the football season. And by late summer, nearly 200 schools from coast to coast had decided to do just that. By mid-July, 189 schools had decided to suspend their football programs for the duration of the war.[1] This epidemic hit every geographic region of the country. Sixty-one schools in the east had dropped the sport along with 49 southern schools, 34 schools in the southwest, 26 schools in the Midwest and 19 in the western United States.

Sure, a large number of those schools that were forced to cancel the season were smaller schools, such as Joe Dienhart's St. Joseph's College in Rennselaer, Ind. But small schools weren't the only ones feeling the strain of the war. Historic programs in the northeast included Harvard, Lafayette, Williams, Wesleyan and Amherst canceled the season. In the southern states, virtually the entire Southeastern Conference called it quits, with Kentucky, Auburn, Mississippi, Mississippi State, Tennessee and Florida suspending the season. And Baylor of the Southwest Conference also canceled its season.

One major reason for schools canceling their season was the fact that the Army's Specialized Training Program had elected not to allow trainees to participate in varsity athletics. The Army's counterpart to the Navy's V-12 program made the decision that trainees wouldn't have time to partake in intercollegiate athletics. Army administrators determined that actual Army bases could form teams and compete as they traditionally had, but the colleges and universities chosen for the special program could not. With ASTP programs at more than 220 institutions around the country, including several that were ultimately forced to cancel their seasons, this was a real blow.[2]

These schools had faced the same circumstances that Purdue had been in back in the early months of 1943. And while many continued to hold out hope that the War Department would reverse their decision in time to salvage the season, even as university presidents and members of Congress petitioned President Roosevelt directly to get involved, it was all to no avail.[3]

While Purdue lucked out when the Navy announced their participation in the V-12 program and the willingness of the program to allow trainees to play sports, many colleges and universities were not as fortunate. By the time the season had rolled around, the Boilermakers had been touched by this trend as well. On August 11th, just a few days after the Purdue men had concluded their summer camp, Michigan State University canceled its season.[4] As a practical matter, this left a hole in the Boilermakers' schedule. Although they would not join the Big Ten conference until 1953, as fate would have it, Purdue was slated to face the Michigan State in West Lafayette on November 13th. The Boilermakers had already been forced to replace a game with Fordham as traveling to New York was out of the question due to regional travel restrictions and the mandate to add Midwestern military installations to the schedule. Incidentally, Fordham would later join the ranks of schools to cancel the season. Now Purdue would be forced to either pick up another opponent just weeks before the beginning of the season or play nine games instead of the regular 10.

Either way, the season would go forward. When the team got back together at the end of August, the focus was clear. They had a very talented opponent to prepare for and less than three weeks in which to do it. The squad would open on the road against Great Lakes Naval Station in Chicago. While playing one of the premier military installations in the country would be a daunting task for any team, it was even more so for a squad of transplanted players who hadn't even known one another six weeks earlier.

As the team began its fall camp, the initial focus was once again on conditioning. Coach Burnham spent the better part of the first two practices on drills and running in order to knock off any rust that may have gathered during the few weeks the team had off from football duties in the month of August.[5] It wasn't until the third practice of the fall session that the Boilermakers started scrimmaging once again.[6] And in the early goings, the aerial game that had been under the tutelage of Cecil Isbell was impressive, as the offensive unit put up three scores through the air, with Sam Vacanti leading the way at quarterback with two of the three tallies while speedy end Joe Buscemi was on the receiving end of all three scores.[7] The possibility of having this potent aerial component was exciting, as previous Boilermaker teams had averaged only about 10 pass attempts per game in the years leading up to 1943. Even better, the summer training sessions were very run-heavy on the offensive side of the ledger. Diversifying the offense by adding a more potent passing game would only help the team succeed.

Isbell began working with the quarterbacks and halfbacks individually, drilling them on the passing game, as the Boilermakers hoped that through innovation and quickness, they might be able to compete with the Great Lakes contingent. The Bluejackets roster would feature various Navy men from around the country, including a handful of former professionals.[8] Furthermore, Great Lakes was getting a chance not only to scrimmage against the NFL's Chicago Cardinals, but would also play the first game of their 1943 season a week before hosting the Boilermakers. This would allow the Bluejackets to potentially work out any kinks well before taking on Purdue, giving an already strong team yet another advantage.[9]

As the days continued to tick away, Burnham decided to have his men practice on Saturday of the first week, a break from convention at the university. Just two weeks remained to prepare for Great Lakes and Burnham continued to make changes amongst three different lineups of players trying to find his best team, although Mother Nature nearly got in the way. Buckets full of rain dumped on the two-hour practice, leaving the field a slippery mess and making evaluation even more difficult.[10]

"We want to give every candidate a chance to prove himself," Burnham told the media following one practice that first week. "However, with Great Lakes as the opening opponent, we are faced with the problem of making somewhat hurried selections."[11]

Burnham's decision on the lineup got a little easier in the second week of practice, but not in a positive way. The lone returning varsity letterman for the Boilermakers, halfback Ed Cycenas, was injured in a scrimmage. Cycenas tore ligaments in his knee and the initial reports put him out for a full three weeks, according to the Purdue training staff. However, when his knee failed to respond to treatment, the leg was put in a cast and the outlook became even more grim.[12] This took an already unclear backfield situation and made it even more muddled. Burnham had a total of twelve halfbacks vying for playing time and Cycenas was the most experienced of the bunch. As Burnham began to put together his traveling squad for the game, a list that would allow just 42 men aboard the train to Chicago, the backfield was bound to be the hardest part to determine. And Burnham knew time was a luxury he didn't have.

"There'll be little time left for experimentation once we launch our schedule," the head man said one day after practice. "Every minute of our somewhat restricted practice time must do double duty."[13]

One thing Burnham was sure about was his desire to open the team's practices up to the public as much as possible. The practice field, located next to the Purdue Fieldhouse on the north end of campus, was open to the public for every practice as long as the fans stayed in the bleachers provided by the university. It was a first for the Purdue program as the coaches focused on not only teaching their team the finer details of football but also on building a fan base amongst the student body and the community. Obviously, with a team made of mostly transfer students, there was very little history between the current players and the community. This openness would go a long way toward building that relationship.[14]

And what they saw at practice was bound to give them hope for a promising season. Because of the Navy's mandate that practices last less than two hours each afternoon, Burnham would often have the squad practice game-like situations through full scrimmages. In the week after Cycenas went down, Lew Rose and Keith Parker emerged as options to take the spot. Rose had earned his freshman numerals in 1942 for the Boilermakers and used his familiarity with the offense to his advantage. Parker, meanwhile, had transferred in from Missouri where he had been a starter in a very similar T-formation offense for the Tigers. Others in the mix included Stan Dubicki, a transfer from Shurtleff College, and Bill Stuart, who was also a Purdue holdover.

Another candidate in the backfield was the newest member of the Boilermaker squad, a transfer from Butler University named Boris "Babe" Dimancheff. The Indianapolis native decided to stay close to home after starring in three sports at George Washington Community High School. Dimancheff was the captain of the freshmen team his first year at Butler and earned all-conference honors as a sophomore in 1942. However, when Butler chose to suspend football in the summer of 1943, Dimancheff was left without a team. He found a new home 70 miles up the road in West Lafayette.

One week before the Boilermakers would kick off their season, they found themselves practicing for the second consecutive Saturday. Burnham continued to try to figure out which players he was taking to Great Lakes for the opener. The practice plan honed in on offensive and defensive drills, with any remaining time spent drilling on special teams. And it was almost exclusively drills at this point rather than full contact scrimmaging as the coaches wanted to make sure the team was as healthy as possible at the start of the season. It also allowed the staff to really focus on the finer details one last time.

Meanwhile, Great Lakes was getting its season of to a good start with a 20-19 win at home over Fort Riley, an Army instillation in Kansas. The sailors drove 67 yards in the opening quarter to take a 6-0 lead. The soldiers answered with 13 points in the second stanza and took a 13-6 lead into the half. Great Lakes answered with a pair of third-quarter touchdowns and led 20-13 in the closing minutes when Fort Riley pushed across their final score. Looking to tie things up with two minutes to play, the PAT was blocked by Great Lakes guard Emil Dvaric and the 20-19 win was preserved.

The Bluejackets dominated the ground game, rushing for 14 first downs and gaining more than 200 yards. Fort Riley had success through the air, with more than 130 yards in the passing game, as they nearly pulled out the comeback. This development could play well into the hands of Purdue, given the time the offense had spent on developing its own aerial attack.

With game week finally upon them, Coach Burnham locked things down a bit around the program. Practice was closed off to the public and by midweek, canvas was wrapped around the fences surrounding the practice field.[15] Forging a bond with the students and the community was all fine and dandy, but game week was game week. Burnham wanted to limit distractions as much as possible.

Purdue didn't have a great history against the squad that resided on the shores of Lake Michigan. Because Great Lakes only fielded a team during times of war, the two programs had faced off only twice prior to 1943, with Great Lakes taking both contests. In 1918, the teams played in Evanston, Ill., on the campus of Northwestern University. Great Lakes, led by future NFL legend George Halas and a host of other college football luminaries, won the game 27-0 en route to an undefeated season and a Rose Bowl championship. In 1942, the Boilermakers hosted Great Lakes at Ross-Ade Stadium. Purdue was defeated 40-0 in that contest, and the Bluejackets went on to claim the national service championship as the best military installation team in the country. Not only had the Boilermakers never defeated the Bluejackets but they had failed to score a single point. Of course, on those two previous occasions, it was the Naval Training Station vs. a group of civilians. This time around, the Boilermakers would have some sailors and Marines of their own.

One distinction the Boilermakers would have on gameday was to be the first civilian team to play at Great Lakes since WWI. After playing the entire 1942 season on the road, Great Lakes had pieced together a home stadium in time for the fall of 1943. Located on the parade grounds of the naval base, Ross Field borrowed a grandstand from the University of Chicago and bleachers from their own baseball stadium to create a capacity of nearly 22,000. And all 22,000 seats were expected to be full of fans for the home team. No tickets were sold and seats were only made available to Navy personnel.[16]

The practice schedule in the week leading up to the opener came together as the Boilermakers spent Monday working on the defense in drills inside the Purdue Fieldhouse. The squad had spent so much time working on offensive installation and trying to determine the backfield that the other side of the ball had gotten short shrift. Finally, some time was spent working on the defense and it would be vital. Assistant coach Joe Dienhart had scouted the Great Lakes opener against Fort Riley and came back with a glowing review of their ground attack.

"Great Lakes has a rugged line working in front of a dangerous backfield," Dienhart reported.[17] He also indicated that Fort Riley had been very opportunistic, turning three fumbles into touchdowns, making the game appear much closer than it was. Great Lakes had dominated the action save for a few early season mistakes.

On Tuesday, Wednesday and Thursday, the Boilermakers moved back outside for practice and boarded a train for Chicago following a light workout Friday afternoon. It was at the Wednesday practice that the Boilermakers had a bit of a revelation…one that could eventually quell the fears of who would start at halfback.

Midway through practice, a group of spectators watching defensive drills noticed a blur of speed at the other end of the field. Team public relations man Bob Woodworth called to Athletic Director Red Mackey, "Come over here and tell me if you see what I see."[18]

The two men took off walking to the offensive side of the field where they realized the flash of speed had been newcomer Babe Dimancheff, taking part in his first scrimmage with the team after joining very late in the process. He had been a Boilermaker for less than two weeks and was still learning the offense, so it wasn't clear how much Dimancheff could contribute against Great Lakes. But it seemed pretty clear he would be a difference maker soon enough. Too bad, too, since the Bluejackets were led by Dimancheff's former coach. Part of the reason Butler had canceled football was that they had lost their head coach to active duty. When Lieutenant Tony Hinkle was activated by the U.S. Navy his assignment to be a coach and instructor at Great Lakes Naval Station.

Burnham put the final touches on his travel roster of 42 men and the lineup appeared to be set. It would be DeFilippo, Agase, Barwegen, Kasap and Genis on the front wall. Buscemi and Bauman would play the end spots and the starting backfield would consist of Vacanti at quarterback, Butkovich at fullback and Rose and Dubicki at the halfback spots.[19]

"I doubt whether we've had time to get really ready for a team of Great Lakes' caliber," said Burnham while announcing his travel roster. "However, this group has displayed a real love for the game and might possibly surprise."[20]

There was one last thing to do before the team headed to the train station on Friday afternoon. Team captains had to be chosen and, fittingly, the men selected for that honor were a pair of V-12 trainees who were getting ready to don the Old Gold and Black for the first time. Tackle John Genis and guard Alex Agase were selected to lead the team onto the field.

A newspaper headline on the morning of gameday brought the reality of the world home to folks in West Lafayette in a very powerful way. The headline announced that Lt. Tom Melton, the captain of the Boilermaker football team in 1941, had been killed in a plane crash while working as a Marine Corps flight instructor. It was an unnecessary reminder for Purdue fans that many things in life, including life itself, are precious.[21]

The team spent the evening at Chicago's Edgewater Beach Hotel on the north side of the city. From there, it was a short trip to Great Lakes Naval Station just up the coast of Lake Michigan where a capacity crowd would watch the action.

A season that had been dominated by uncertainty, that nearly didn't happen, began in about as poor a fashion as it could've for the Boilermakers. Purdue received the opening kick and on the second play from scrimmage, a mix-up between Vacanti and Butkovich led to a fumble a quick turnover. Great Lakes scored two plays later and, with the season less than two minute old, it appeared to already be going sideways for Purdue. Was 1943 to be more of the same? Was it too much to expect a roster full of transplanted players to form a cohesive unit? Was the preseason hope all a mirage?

Their next possession saw the Boilermakers gain just one first down before punting. Then the fumble bug switched sides as Frank Bauman recovered a loose ball and the Purdue offense was in business near midfield. The Boilermakers went 42 yards in nine plays with Butkovich crashing over the goal line for the 7-6 lead. Burnham sent in a fresh lineup to start the second quarter, 11 new players to run the offense and they wasted little time with a quick touchdown drive capped off by a 23-yard scoring run by halfback Bill Stuart. The reserve running back from Hammond, Ind., broke several tackles on the way to the end zone.

After the Bluejackets began to move the ball on their next drive, Burnham sent the starters back in on defense and the threat was quickly nullified. The score remained 13-6 at the half. The Boilermakers added a field goal in the third quarter and was firmly in control headed to the final frame.

The teams exchanged punts before Great Lakes once again was able to put together an offensive drive. Fullback Ken Roskie plunged into the end zone for a score and halfway through the fourth quarter, the Purdue lead was cut to 16-13.

Great Lakes got the ball back after Jimmy Darr threw an interception deep in Great Lakes territory. The Bluejackets appeared to have momentum and nearly took the game over. A long attempt from Great Lakes fell incomplete at midfield after receiver Steve Juzwik dropped a wind-open pass. The home fans groaned and the Boilermaker sideline breathed a sigh of relief. The defense held and forced a punt.

Stan Dubicki waited at midfield to receive the punt for the Boilermakers and he turned in his finest return of the day, sprinting 33 yards down to the 12. On fourth down from the five-yard line, with time running out and his team clinging to a three-point lead, Coach Burnham passed on the field goal attempt. He let his offense go in for the kill and Dubicki delivered, swinging around the right end and outrunning the defense to the corner flag for the final score of the day. The Boilermakers were victorious 23-13.

Purdue outgained Great Lakes 166 to 40 on the ground and while the Bluejackets had the better passing attack, it largely came in the second half when they were playing catch up. The Boilermaker defense forced four turnovers on the day and Purdue was penalized just once for five yards. As expected, the front line earned most of the postgame praise for their effort. Not only did the crew clear the way for the offense for most of the day, they repeatedly turned away the Great Lakes efforts while playing on the defensive side of the ball. It was expected that the line would be the strength of the ball club. They didn't disappoint.

Some questioned, however, if the Boilermakers were really good or if Great Lakes was somewhat overrated. Well, both teams would have a chance to answer those questions as the season continued to unfold. For Purdue, some answers were now less than a week away as they prepared to head to Milwaukee to take on what appeared to be a very good Marquette team.

CHAPTER 8

| WEEK TWO |
AT MARQUETTE

In 1942, the Marquette Golden Avalanche had a very good season, finishing with a record of 7-2. The small Jesuit school in Milwaukee, Wisc., wasn't a traditional power, certainly not on the level of other independents in the Midwest but they had had some success. The program played its first game in 1892 and took part in the inaugural Cotton Bowl in 1937. Most seasons they were an also-ran ball club but under second-year head coach Thomas Stidham, the 1942 squad showed real promise. Four of their seven wins were by way of a shutout and their two losses came at the hands of national champion Wisconsin and service school national champ Great Lakes. With eight returning letter-winners back for the 1943 season, there was a great nucleus to build upon. But beyond that, there was even more room for optimism.

Marquette had also been selected to serve as a V-12 training program, welcoming future officers seeking training in engineering and pre-medical/pre-dental areas. In early July, nearly 800 future Navy officers stepped foot on campus for the first time. Father Raphael

McCarthy, the president of Marquette University, welcomed the new Navy men along with more than 300 Army trainees seeking medical training. Just like the other schools around the nation selected to take part in these programs, the influx of military personnel was a boon to the university. Of course, correlating with that influx of personnel was a huge increase in potential players for Coach Stidham and company.

Now, since Marquette offered only two training areas within the V-12 program, several Marine trainees who had been at the university were transferred to a different institution. For Marquette, that designated school was Notre Dame and several players from the 1942 team were now members of the Fighting Irish squad. At least seven Marquette veterans joined the Irish due to Navy transfer orders. But the Golden Avalanche had its share of experience coming in as well. More than 40 men on his opening day roster were made of transfers from other universities including former Ivy League stars from Brown and Yale and a few Big Ten transfers. From Indiana University came Chuck Chesbro, who earned his freshman numerals with the Hoosiers in 1942. And from Purdue University came Bill Combs.[1]

* * * * *

Loyal William Combs arrived at Purdue in the fall of 1938 after starring in football and basketball at Lowell High School while also finishing at the top of his graduating class. After a year of playing freshman football for then-freshman coach Elmer Burnham, Combs was a star end for the Purdue varsity. In his senior season, Combs earned All-Big Ten honors and was selected as the team's MVP. In the spring of 1942, Combs was drafted by the Philadelphia Eagles, playing in 10 games for the Eagles in the '42 season.

Combs joined the Navy with an eye toward medical training and the V-12 program shipped him to Marquette because of its pre-medical program. He studied to be a medic and after the war returned to Marquette to complete medical school. "Doc" Combs headed back home to Lowell, Ind., after graduation and began a private practice. But he could never quite get away from his past in athletics. He spent a decade as an assistant football coach and the team physician at his old high school while running his practice.

In 1956, Combs returned to his original alma mater to become the director of the student hospital on campus and the team physician for Purdue Athletics. "Doc" Combs would serve as the team doctor for the Boilermakers for the next 40 years, earning great respect within the athletic training world. He served as a team doctor for Team USA at several international competitions throughout the course of his career and in 1997 was a member of the inaugural class of the Purdue Intercollegiate Athletics Hall of Fame. But in early September 1943, thanks to the Navy's V-12 program and his future in medicine, he was preparing to suit up on the other sideline.

* * * * *

As the Boilermakers gathered to begin preparing for Marquette, the joy of the season-opening win over Great Lakes was short-lived. After all, the Golden Avalanche squad had an impressive season-opener of their own, going on the road to take dismantle in-state rival Wisconsin 33-7. And while the Badgers were a vastly different team than the squad that shared the national title in 1942, it was still a great win for Marquette. Now they would be returning home for their home-opener, a night game versus yet another Big Ten opponent.

Burnham and the coaching staff set out to correct the mistakes the team had made in the opener at Great Lakes. There were a few early season rough spots that needed to be smoothed out. Turnovers were a concern as they can make a good Saturday turn bad very quickly. And the passing game was nowhere near as effective as the offensive minds wanted it to be. Meanwhile, on the other side of the ball, far too much was surrendered through the air allowing the Bluejackets to hang around in the second half.

Burnham also continued to try and figure out which backfield combination was the right one for his ball club. It appeared Butkovich had locked up the fullback spot, gaining 85 yards on 17 carries in the opener. But the two halfback slots were still up for grabs. Several players had good moments in the opener with Bill Stuart and Stan Dubicki both finding the end zone. Babe Dimancheff also found some success in his limited action and Lew Rose, Keith Parker and others earned playing time as well. One thing seemed certain, however, as injured halfback Ed Cycenas would miss another week.

"Anything can happen," said Burnham following Tuesday night's practice. "There apparently is little to choose between the two teams."[2]

Burnham's counterpart had much stronger opinions about the matchup when talking with the press.

"They're two touchdowns better than us, but they'll have to fight for them," Stidham said. "There is no danger of our boys being overconfident because of their one-sided victory over Wisconsin. All of us know we face a terrific battle here Saturday night."[3]

The travel squad set, the Boilermakers had a light practice on Friday afternoon and then headed to the train station. The plan once again was to travel as far as Chicago, spend the night, then finish the trip on Saturday morning. There would be one addition to the itinerary for week two however.

The team had a stop at the Purdue Memorial Union on the way to the Big Four station in downtown Lafayette. A group of more than 250 students and supporters had turned out for the season's first pep rally to send the team off. A steady rain dampened the festivities a bit, canceling the planned appearance of the university's All-American Marching Band, but the Boilermaker Special led the procession across the levee to the station. Cheerleaders and supporters kept everyone's spirits up even as the rain delayed the departure of the team's train by nearly an hour.[4]

Any apprehension the Boilermakers may have felt headed into the game was only heightened by a capacity crowd at Marquette Stadium under the lights. When the game kicked off at 8 p.m. nearly 23,000 fans had packed into the stadium, the largest crowd to watch a college game in the city's history. Marquette selected former Boilermaker Bill Combs to serve as captain and he led his new squad onto the field to face his former team.[5]

The Boilermakers got over whatever nerves they had pretty quickly, receiving the opening kickoff and promptly driving 71 yards for the game's opening score. Burnham and his staff put together a game-plan that allowed his team to simply dominate. There were no frills, none of the trick plays or deception they had spent time working on throughout the week. Just straight ahead, meat-and-potatoes football. The opening drive saw Purdue pound the ball up the middle repeatedly, with Butkovich and Dimancheff routinely breaking multiple tackles on runs. On a play that typified the drive, Butkovich took an inside handoff from Vacanti and blasted through initial contact at the line, then slipped an attempted tackle by the Marquette middle linebacker before a second linebacker and a safety had to combine to bring him down 12 yards downfield. Three plays later, "Touchdown Tony" earned the final three yards for the score and a 7-0 lead.

Marquette received the ensuing kickoff and returned it to the 32-yard line. But the tone for the evening was set on their first offensive snap of the game. A shotgun snap came to Marquette quarterback Ollie Vogt and, as he attempted a bit of misdirection, five Boilermaker defenders were on top of him for a seven-yard loss. A second-down run went nowhere and a third-down pass fell incomplete but the drive was kept alive by a Purdue penalty. Still, after three more plays that went nowhere, it was a quick punt for the Hilltoppers.

Vacanti was intercepted on the next Purdue drive and Marquette had its starting field position of the day as the first quarter ended. They drove down to the Purdue 17-yard line before three consecutive passes fell incomplete and they turned the ball over on downs. Once again it was time for the Purdue offensive line to take control while Butkovich, Dimancheff and Stuart combined to drive the ball 50 yards on the ground without a single pass play being called. Coach Burnham started to mix up the point of attack with wide sweeps and inside counters sprinkled here and there, but it was still 12 straight run plays for the Boilermakers. And when Sam Vacanti finally dropped back to throw, he found Frank Bauman at the 15, who took care of the rest, crossing the goal line to take a 14-0 lead into the half. Marquette had gained just five yards on the ground in the first half and had its only scoring threat because of a Purdue interception rather than anything the offense had done.

The teams traded turnovers in a scoreless third quarter and Dimancheff closed out the scoring with a 13-yard touchdown, his first for the Boilermakers. Babe took a handoff and followed the block of left guard Dick Barwegen for about five yards before veering hard to the right and finding a wide-open running lane to the end zone. Purdue closed out a 21-0 victory that was far more dominant than the final score might indicate.

The Boilermaker offense finished with 210 yards on the ground and more than 300 yards of total offense. The passing game did enough, completing 6 of 12 for 98 yards as the offense earned 14 first downs in the game. The real masterpiece was turned in by the Purdue defense, though, as it gave up just 108 total yards and forced three turnovers in the shutout. Marquette ran for just 44 yards on the day and earned just six first downs total. Every man who made the trip north for Purdue saw game action except for the injured Cycenas, with the team's third-string playing the bulk of the fourth quarter.

After the game, praise for the Boilermaker effort came from all corners. In the hotel lobby that Saturday night following the game, Coach Burnham was seen celebrating with alumni and fans. Burnham and his coaching staff had earned the adulation of Boilermakers everywhere with the hard work not just in the Marquette victory but in the six months leading up to the season. There was plenty left to do but they took a few moments to enjoy this dominant win.

After the game, one alumnus had very strong and meaningful praise. Bill Combs met with reporters and spoke glowingly about his former team. "I believe that's the best college football team I ever played against," Combs said.[6]

One of his opponents wholeheartedly agreed.

"I know I played with some good lines at Fordham," said Purdue center Lou DeFilippo. "But I believe this line at Purdue is better than any of them."[7]

Some folks on the national stage were beginning to take notice as well. Two wins over what were expected to be powerful programs in 1943 had garnered Purdue some attention. The first United Press regional poll of the season placed the Boilermakers first in the Midwest, ahead of Michigan and Notre Dame.[8] The Associated Press had issued a small notice as well, letting readers know not to forget about the Boilermakers, though the season's first A.P. Poll was still over a week away.

The team boarded the train back to campus on Sunday morning and arrived at the station to find a few hundred supporters had turned out to welcome the victors home. With rallies bookending the successful trip north, there could be no doubting the support the squad was getting from the community. And they'd need it, too, as Purdue was scheduled to begin the Big Ten season next, and at home no less. The opponent? Well, it was a familiar one. And for several men on the squad, it was far too familiar. Illinois was coming to town and for a dozen Purdue players, it would be the most difficult game of their career. They had to suit up against their former team, their former coach and, for one Boilermaker, an actual brother.

CHAPTER 9

| WEEK THREE |
VS. ILLINOIS

When considering the biggest rivals in the Big Ten Conference, one gets pretty far down the list before arriving at Purdue vs. Illinois. In fact, you could argue each program has a bigger rival within their own state borders. Geographically, less than 100 miles separate the two campuses and there are a lot of similarities between the two universities. Both were founded as Land-Grant institutions within just a few years of each other just after the Civil War. Both were built on the basis of strong agriculture, science and engineering programs, as required by the Morrill Act of 1862, signed by President Abraham Lincoln, himself a figure claimed by both Indiana and Illinois.

On the gridiron, Purdue and Illinois first faced off in November 1890, with the Boilermakers taking the contest 62-0. The teams played 26 more times in the next 40 years, with the Fighting Illini getting the better of the series, posting 14-8-4 record over the Boilermakers. And then, following the 1931 contest, the series stopped. For more than a decade, the teams didn't play each other on the gridiron. Peculiarities in Big Ten scheduling found teams playing between four and six conference games during that time frame and both schools fostered other rivalries. The Fighting Illini played regular series throughout the 1930s with Notre Dame, USC and Washington University in St. Louis. The Boilermakers, meanwhile, headed east with yearly matchups with Carnegie Tech in Pittsburgh and Fordham University in the Bronx.

With the rivalry being renewed in the 1943 season, alumni groups thought it appropriate to mark the occasion by introducing a new traveling trophy to be awarded to the winner. And they had the perfect symbol for the rivalry: the Purdue Cannon, the origin story for which could seemingly only happen in American collegiate athletics.

* * * * *

In October 1905, a group of Purdue students headed to Champaign for the matchup between the two teams. The visiting students brought with them a small, muzzle-loading cannon with the intent of firing it after a Boilermaker win. They hid the cannon in a culvert near the field and were anxious to light the fuse following a 29-0 win by their Purdue squad. However, during the game, the cannon was discovered by an Illinois undergraduate named Quincy A. "Buddy" Hall. Hall and a group of his Delta Upsilon fraternity brothers confiscated the cannon and carried it back to their house.[1]

That's where it stayed until Hall relocated the Purdue Cannon to his family farm in Milford, Ill. Hall graduated in 1907 with a degree in engineering and spent more than 30 years working in the field, including seven years working in Panama at the time of the construction of the Panama Canal. He then returned to the farm in Milford. After several decades of the relic collecting dust, Hall decided it was time to reintroduce it to the public, reaching out to offer it as a traveling trophy for the rivals. After much discussion, it was decided Hall would travel to West Lafayette on gameday and, at halftime, would present the trophy to athletic directors Doug Mills of Illinois and Red Mackey of Purdue.[2]

* * * * *

The new trophy was a nice bonus for the competitors but there was absolutely no need for extra motivation for this particular game. The Boilermakers were riding high after two big wins to start the season over what were considered by most to be strong opponents. The Fighting Illini, meanwhile, were still looking for their first win after falling to Camp Grant and Iowa Pre-Flight, two military instillations similar to the Great Lakes Naval group Purdue had opened the season against. And there was the little matter of the Purdue team being loaded with former Fighting Illini players.

The early-season success the Boilermakers were having could fairly be attributed, almost exclusively, to former Illini players Alex Agase, John Genis, Mike Kasap, Frank Bauman, Joe Buscemi and Tony Butkovich. All had started both games thus far and all had made major contributions in those wins. In fact, the student newspaper at Illinois, *The Daily Illini*, had taken to referring to the Boilermaker squad as "Purd-Illini" in the lead up to the game. It was going to be a very tough challenge for the Illinois, going up against a squad they knew so well. And it was only necessary because of administrative decisions made the previous spring, far away from campus and well out of their hands.

The University of Illinois had applied for and been accepted inclusion as a V-12 Training institution. However, when those selections had been made, the school in central Illinois was designated as a center for Engineering and Pre-Medical/Pre-Dental trainees only. Of the 131 V-12 institutions across the country, just 39 had been designated as training centers for future Marines and they were fairly evenly distributed geographically. In the Midwest, Northwestern University, the University of Michigan, the University of Notre Dame and Purdue University had become destinations for Marine trainees.

Because of the speed and scale surrounding all of these decisions, there was confusion through the spring and it wasn't until early summer that the dust settled. Marine trainees from the University of Illinois finally got their transfer orders and the Fighting Illini football team was decimated by the decision with five letter-winners being sent to Notre Dame for training and nine being shipped to Purdue. When the University of Illinois' V-12 program opened on July 1 with 450 future naval officers, their Marines were gone.

Just weeks earlier, before the final transfer decisions had been announced, the Illinois coaching staff were sitting around their offices when Alex Agase and Tony Butkovich walked in. The two had become great friends as teammates on the football field and on the Illinois wrestling team. On this day in May, Alex and Tony had a third with them and he was the reason for the drop-in.

"Hey, you guys," Butkovich said. "I want you to meet my brother Bill."

"I'm glad to see there's one good looking boy in the Butkovich family," replied athletics department business manager Bud Lyon. "Are you gonna come down here to school, Bill?"

"Yeah, I've been planning on going to school," replied the younger Butkovich brother. "Probably here, I'm just about sure. I won't start until August."

"You have a brother, too, don't you Aggie," asked (assistant coach Vic) Heyliger.

"I do," replied Agase. "His name's Lou. He's probably going here or Northwestern."[3]

The coaching staff didn't like the sound of that and let Agase know it with light-hearted boo's. Shortly after, the bell rang and the two Illinois undergrads hurried off to class, little brother Bill in tow. Six weeks later, Alex and Tony were no longer members of Coach Ray Eliot's squad, though that didn't mean the affection between the men ceased.

Agase and Butkovich met up to drive to Purdue together at the end of June and made a pit stop along the way. Champaign wasn't much of a detour on the way to West Lafayette and, before long, the two men found themselves back on campus at the University of Illinois. With summer practices having already commenced on the fields just outside of Memorial Stadium, stopping by to say hello to Coach Eliot and his new squad seemed like the thing to do.

As Alex and Tony got out of their car and walked across the practice field, Coach Eliot saw his two stars in street clothes and gave a smile. Eliot stopped his team's drills and had everyone gather round. The squad of more than three dozen youngsters were mostly freshmen or newcomers and he needed to introduce his guests.

"Men, I want to introduce a couple members from last year's team," Eliot began. "Tony Butkovich is the finest fullback of his size in the country. He's going to be a tough man to stop this fall. And this here is Alex Agase, the finest lineman in the country. Aggie was an All-

American for us last year and will be even better this fall."

"You've got a good lookin' squad here, Ray," replied Butkovich. "I'd give anything to join you fellas this fall."

"And you boys have the best coaching staff in the country, bar none," added Agase. "The only secret to you having a great season is to listen closely and do exactly what they tell you to do."[4]

With that, Eliot ordered his team back to action and bid farewell to his guests. His former players watched for a few minutes longer then headed back to the car, to the rest of their road trip and to their new team.

With the first two wins in the books, the Purdue squad was really starting to hit its stride. Offensively, the backfield had finally seemed to be solidified with Butkovich the emerging star at fullback and Dimancheff putting a stranglehold on one of the halfback positions that had been up for grabs. The front line was widely believed to be among the best in the country and the defense was gaining a reputation of being absolutely stifling, having surrendered just 90 yards on the ground through the season's first two games.

Coming off two road trips and with all of the demands on his players off the field, Coach Elmer Burnham took a bit of a different approach to practice in the lead-up to the Illinois game. The first few days of the week were devoted more to scouting the Illinois personnel and formations with some lighter physical work. Burnham warned his boys not to take the Illini lightly no matter their record.

"Any team that can score three touchdowns on the Iowa Seahawks is a dangerous foe," warned Burnham, referring to Illinois' most recent game, a 32-18 loss to Iowa Pre-Flight. "Illinois has two weeks to prepare for us and it's a great spot for an upset."[5]

As the Boilermakers studied what they knew of the Fighting Illini squad, they had no clue that their preparation was an exercise in futility. Coach Eliot had decided to put his two weeks off to good use by installing a brand new offensive system. For the first time, Illinois would be employing a T-formation just like Purdue. Banking on the formation's ability to showcase experienced halfbacks Eddie Bray and Eddie McGovern, Eliot quietly installed the new offense to try and gain the element of surprise against the Purdue squad that knew his old system as well as anyone could.[6]

Another problem the Boilermakers had was in scouting Illinois personnel. There was a bit of a revolving door for the Fighting Illini early in the season with new players arriving and veterans leaving. Team captain Bob Prymuski played the first two games while on furlough from his post in the Army but returned to active duty and stepped away from the gridiron after the game against Iowa Pre-Flight. Five new men joined the Fighting Illini in the week leading up to the Purdue game.[7]

The Fighting Illini, meanwhile, had ample opportunity to scout the Boilermakers. In fact, Eliot himself was able to scout Purdue for the Marquette game. Because the Illini were off that Saturday, he drove to Madison, Wisc., to catch the afternoon tilt between Wisconsin and Camp Grant then headed to Milwaukee to watch the nightcap between the Boilermakers and Marquette.

After the game, Coach Eliot actually ran into a few of his former players. Following Purdue's shutout victory, Eliot saw Agase, John Genis and Mike Kasap and was able to chat with them for a few moments. "You guys look like a gang of pros out there," Eliot said in shadows of Marquette Stadium after the game.

"Wait until you see us next week, coach," replied Kasap.[8]

No doubt, Eliot was already having trouble sleeping because of that prospect. He wasn't the only one with conflicting emotions. A few days before the game, Butkovich was asked if it would be difficult facing off against his old mates. The bruising fullback smiled and replied, "Brother, this is war!".[9] It was an ironic statement for a few reasons. It wasn't lost on anyone that of course it wasn't war…it was a game. But a game brought on only because of a war. Also, the first word in his response spoke volumes. Younger brother Bill, whom Tony had introduced to the Illinois coaching staff some five months earlier, had, in fact, enrolled at the university. He would wear the orange and blue and he chose the same numerals as big brother, wearing the #25 jersey. And thanks to the ruling by the NCAA and the Big Ten to relax eligibility restrictions, Bill would be able to play against big brother Saturday despite being just a freshman.

The All-American Marching Band led the first official pep rally of the season with a march from the Memorial Union to Stuart Field on Friday evening. Revelers fell in line behind them with signs and torches along the way. Upon arrival, hundreds of fans enjoyed a bonfire and music along with speeches from university President Edward C. Elliott, athletics director Red Mackey and Purdue coaches

Elmer Burnham and Cecil Isbell.[10] The stage was set for the next afternoon's rivalry to commence.

For the third week in a row, Agase and Genis were selected by Burnham to lead the Boilermakers as the captains for the game. Of course, they were facing their former mates so it was a significant choice. Even more interesting, Genis was supposed to be the man leading the Illini onto the field. At the conclusion of the 1942 season, the Chicago native was elected captain for the 1943 Illinois squad.

A sunshine-filled afternoon welcomed more than 15,000 spectators to Ross-Ade Stadium on gameday and the contest they witnessed was one they would not soon forget, although not necessarily for the right reasons. The two teams combined for 20 fumbles on the day and an astonishing 19 turnovers as each squad took turns trying to let the other run away with it, only to be denied.

Illinois received the opening kick and promptly turned the ball over. The opening five minutes of the game saw five turnovers alone as the teams kept exchanging fumbles. Finally, Sam Vacanti dropped back to pass for the Boilermakers and found an open Joe Buscemi to break the scoreless tie. Running back Eddie Bray fumbled on the Fighting Illini's next possession and Agase recovered deep in Illinois territory. Three plays later, Tony Butkovich plunged into the end zone from three yards out, thanks to a devastating block from backfield mate Babe Dimancheff, and the Boilermakers had a 14-0 lead in the opening moments of the second quarter.

As had become his custom, Burnham began the second quarter with the second string, a tactic he had adopted from his coaching mentor Knute Rockne to try wearing down an opponent with fresh forces. However, Illinois had instant success, moving the ball at will against the second team, leading Burnham to reverse course after just a few minutes and reinsert the starters. This drew some derisive comments from the Illinois reporters up in the press box, as they interpreted the move as a slap in the face against their team. Their comments were a bit out of place when they made them and would be downright silly by the end of the game as Burnham repeatedly showed respect to the Fighting Illini, refusing to run the score up. But with a two score lead early in the second quarter, the Boilermaker coach felt the tide shifting and made a move.

The Purdue defense stood tall and forced a punt which McGovern put through the end zone. On the first play of the ensuing possession,

Butkovich broke loose. Taking a pitch from Vacanti on a sweep around the left end, Tony outran a would-be tackler in the backfield, then busted through two defenders at the 25-yard line. Tony kept going. He broke another tackle at the 35 and ran through the arms of a fourth defender at the 40. At this point, he picked up some help. Agase threw a block from his knees, taking out an Illinois defender, and Genis took two men down with one block. Suddenly at midfield, Tony found himself five yards in front of the nearest defender. That's as close as they got as Touchdown Tony turned on the jets and finished off the 80-yard scoring gallop. Purdue ran its lead to 21-0.

The reserves came in to close out the second quarter and the teams resumed trading turnovers. Illinois finally pushed the ball across the goal line just before the end of the half, aided in large part by a Purdue pass interference call, and the halftime score read Purdue 21, Illinois 7.

After the halftime Cannon Dedication ceremony, the Boilermakers received the opening kick, which Bill Stuart fumbled. The Boilermakers caught a break as Illinois had a touchdown pass nullified thanks to a call for an illegal block in the back. Purdue also had a long touchdown called back in the third quarter thanks to a penalty but late in the period, Stan Dubicki took a pitch around the right end and scampered 53-yards untouched for the 27-7 lead. Another Illini fumble led to Butkovich covering 23 yards on two carries and crashing in for his third score on the day to give Purdue a 34-7 lead.

The game seemingly in hand, Burnham decided to try to sit the first team for the rest of the game, giving playing time to the second and third stringers. The dominance of his starters was well established and with so many close connections between the teams, there was no need to embarrass anyone. This decision came despite the protestations of several of his former Illini players. Agase, Butkovich, Buscemi and several others were openly frustrated with being pulled out of the game, especially with things going so well.

Their displeasure didn't last long as a few of the men decided to take advantage of the down time in a pretty unique way. Butkovich, Agase and Genis made their way to the visiting sideline to visit with their old compatriots. Butkovich stayed for just a brief time then returned to the Purdue sideline but Agase and Genis made themselves at home on the Illinois bench, two white jerseys surrounded by a sea of blue and orange.

On the field the mistakes continued to pile up for the Boilermakers with turnovers, penalties and a blocked punt that the Fighting Illini pounced on in the end zone for a score. Midway through the fourth quarter, the score 34-14, Eddie Bray got loose for Illinois and squeezed through a hole in the middle of the Purdue defense, cut right and sprinted 70 yards for a score. With the score now 34-21 and six minutes remaining in the game, Burnham decided to put his starters back in. At that, Agase and Genis stood up on the Illinois sideline, said so long to their former teammates and rejoined their current squad on the field. Burnham's decision took all of two plays to pay off.

Quarterback Sam Vacanti fielded the Illinois kickoff at his own 30 and took off. After a 45-yard return by the former Iowa Hawkeye signal caller, the Purdue offense was in great position, first and ten from the Illinois 25. Dimancheff went in motion-left from his right halfback position and at the snap, Vacanti handed off the Butkovich. Tony headed wide left, got solid blocks from Dubicki and Dimancheff, then followed a convoy of blockers led by Kasap and Genis across the goal line for his fourth score on the day. That put the finishing touches on a 40-21 final score.

On the day, in addition to his four touchdowns, Butkovich was absolutely prolific. He finished with a school-record 207 yards on just 12 carries, good for an average of 17.3 yards per carry. He now had six touchdowns in three games, tops in the Big Ten. As a team the Boilermakers rushed for 403 yards and, if not for the turnovers and penalties, would've been in line for significantly more. Bray, meanwhile, finished with 132 yards on the ground for the Fighting Illini in a fine performance of his own.

In a moment that no doubt made their parents, Blaz and Anna Butkovich, proud, the Butkovich brothers had a chance to square off in the contest. It wasn't a new thing for the boys as Tony and Bill went to different high schools and had grown up playing against each other on occasion. But never at this level. So, when Bill came in to play defensive back in the third quarter, it was special. When he tackled his big brother on his first play in the game, it was even better. The public-address announcer let it be known that a special moment had just occurred, blaring "Butkovich just tackled Butkovich" for all to hear.[11] Tackling Tony was really a rarity that afternoon, as Bill would soon learn as well. He had a front row seat to Tony's third and fourth touchdowns as big brother ran right at him each time.

Praise for the Boilermakers was universal from the Fighting Illini players in the visiting locker room. Several commented after the game that the front seven was the best they'd seen and end Joe Buscemi was singled out as a special talent. Eddie McGovern commented, "They were all tough. All over the field. And those ends are two of the best I'd seen. I don't think you could get Buscemi down."[12]

Meanwhile, in the Purdue locker room, a very special scene was unfolding. Agase and Butkovich, Genis and Kasap and all the rest of the former Illini players now wearing the colors of Purdue huddled together...with Illinois coach Ray Eliot.

"Where'd you get that 'T'," shouted Agase when Eliot entered the room. "Boy it sure had us fooled for a while. We knew you'd have something up your sleeve, Ray. That's why we were more afraid of you than we were Great Lakes or Marquette."

"Yeah, I know," laughed Eliot. "It's too bad I taught Kasap how to cover the flank on those T-formation sweeps last year. It all comes back to get me now!"[13]

The group carried on for a while, eventually joined by longtime Illinois trainer Matt Bullock. Butkovich stood there cradling the game ball with a big grin on his face. Prior to the game, Burnham had promised game balls to him and Genis if the Boilermakers won the contest and the coach had delivered. Tony was happy to have played so well, sure, but just as happy to have been able to face off against his brother. "He's gonna be alright," said Tony, referencing the hard hit he absorbed from young Bill in the second half.[14]

"You know, they almost handed me the ball once," said Agase, playing on a running gag between the lineman and his former head coach. On numerous occasions during the previous season, Agase had teased his coach about needing to carry the ball or threatening to have running backs lateral the ball to him during plays.

"That's all we needed," replied Eliot. "To get beat by a couple of more touchdowns."[15]

After a bit more visiting the Illini brethren bid adieu to their former players and headed to their cars for the drive back across state lines. The Boilermakers celebrated into the night, savoring what might be the sweetest victory of this special season, once they got used to the slight bitterness of it. But the celebration wouldn't last too long. After all, there was another opponent to get ready for.

CHAPTER 10

| WEEK FOUR |
VS. CAMP GRANT

Camp Grant Army base was founded on the outskirts of Rockford, Ill., with the United States' entry into World War I in 1917 and it had a colorful history. Named for the legendary General Ulysses Grant, himself a long-time inhabitant of the region, the base served initially as one of the largest training facilities in the U.S. Army. It was the birthplace of the 86th Infantry Division, the Blackhawk Division. In late 1918, a breakout of the Spanish Flu infected some 4,000 soldiers at the base, killing more than 1,000 of them. Shortly after The Great War ended, the encampment was turned over to the Illinois National Guard. However, the U.S. Army reactivated the base in February 1941, converting it into an Army Medical Service training center.

By the fall of 1943, Camp Grant was not only serving as a medical training facility and a regional basic training location but had also become a Prisoner of War camp, serving as the temporary home for several thousand mostly German prisoners captured on the battlefield.[1.] Camp Grant was one of more than 500 POW camps that sprouted up around the country to house combatants for the duration of the war. Oftentimes the prisoners would be loaned out to area factories to help the manpower shortage and local farms to assist with planting and harvesting seasons. When the war concluded, the prisoners returned to Europe, though many eventually returned to America.[2]

Also of note in the fall of 1943 was the football team made up of soldiers on base. The Camp Grant team had formed in 1942, putting together a 4-5 record. The constant movement of personnel meant that the squad in 1943 would scarcely resemble to previous year's team, starting with a new coach. Former Michigan State head man Charlie Bachmann had left East Lansing after the 1942 season and volunteered to be the coach for the Warriors. Bachmann had already distinguished himself with success at Kansas State, Florida and Michigan State and was quite a get for the Camp Grant squad.

Bachmann had an experienced team made up of soldiers who had starred previously in college and the NFL. The front line consisted of players formerly of the Pittsburgh Steelers and Washington Redskins as well as regulars from Indiana, Notre Dame and Colgate. The backfield featured quarterback Reino Nori, who had spent time with the Chicago Bears and the Detroit Lions, along with former Purdue players Bill Burghardt and John Andretich, who had played for the Boilermakers in the early 1940s.[3,4]

Camp Grant was off to a good start in the 1943 season with a 2-1-1 record against competition very similar to what the Boilermakers had faced. The Warriors opened the campaign with a 23-0 shutout of Illinois in Champaign. That was followed by a loss at home to a powerful Michigan team. The Warriors then defeated Wisconsin 10-7 and tied Marquette 7-7, using scoring drives in the closing minutes of both games to ensure positive results. One thing was certain, it was not shaping up to be a walk in the park for the Boilermakers when they welcomed Camp Grant to Ross-Ade Stadium.

The Boilermakers continued to garner national attention for their dominant performances and when the season's first Associated Press poll came out the week of the Camp Grant game, it had the undefeated Boilermakers ranked as No. 7 in the country, the first poll appearance for Purdue since assistant coach Cecil Isbell's junior season in 1936. What's more, the Boilermakers received two votes for the top spot.[5]

Purdue assistant coach Joe Dienhart had the task of scouting the Warrior squad and spoke very plainly about the challenge. "We're going to be up against a tough proposition," Dienhart said at a practice early in the week, citing the fact that the Warrior front line averaged 216 pounds per man, a solid 10-20 pounds more per man than the Purdue front.[6]

Ball security was the focus at Monday afternoon's practice, the coaches knowing the team had dodged a bullet after putting the ball on the ground ten times vs. Illinois and still emerging victorious. Drills stayed light early in the week, as had become customary for the ball club.

There was no history between Purdue and Camp Grant. The two teams had never played before and would never play again. And unlike the week before when connections were plentiful between the team and the opposition, there was precious little between these groups. But the game had taken on some added significance for one Boilermaker.

Starting center Lou DeFilippo had met with head coach Elmer Burnham prior to the Illinois game and the two men hashed out Lou's future. They agreed that the former New York Giant, who had played with distinction for three seasons at Fordham University, had played more than one man's share of collegiate ball. DiFilippo and Burnham decided that it would only be fair for him to play against fellow military teams. He sat out the Illinois game, though his absence certainly hadn't affected the outcome. And the contest against Camp Grant would be his final game for the Boilermakers.[7]

DiFilippo had enlisted in the Navy in the summer of 1942 and attained the rank of Chief Specialist. After being transferred to Purdue, he worked on his Master's Degree in physical education and was an instructor for other Navy men. That was exactly the role he had taken on the team as well, spending a majority of his time teaching younger and less experienced teammates the finer points of interior line play. On the defensive side of the ball he was often the catalyst calling the plays and on the offensive side he had a calming presence for the whole unit. DiFilippo would certainly be missed and his teammates wanted to send him out right.

As the game kicked off, it was clear the size advantage was with the Warriors and of course they had more experience than their Purdue counterparts. But the Boilermaker front wall played like a unit on a mission, as if they collectively took all the talk about the Warrior front wall as a personal affront. Camp Grant received the opening kick and returned it to the 28-yard line. The Boilermakers stuffed a first down run for a loss of a yard and, in an attempt to gain the field position advantage, the Warriors called for a quick punt on second down. Jimmy Dewar, the former Indiana Hoosier halfback and future Cleveland Brown, took the snap and before he could get his rhythm, Alex Agase, John Genis and Dick Barwegen swarmed him. The trickery hadn't actually tricked anyone on the Purdue defensive line. It was unclear which of the Boilermakers blocked the punt, only that one of them had and Frank Bauman hopped on the ball at the 24-yard line.

On their first offensive snap, the Boilermakers decided to pull a little deception of their own. Sam Vacanti called out a signal and the backfield shifted. After acting like the shift had been messed up, the backfield shifted back to its original T-formation and, on a silent count, DiFilippo snapped the ball. Stan Dubicki streaked toward the sideline from his left halfback position and Vacanti zipped a pass to him in the flat. Dubicki weaved through two flat-footed defenders and sprinted 24 yards to the end zone for the opening score. Purdue had kicked off, created a turnover and scored and less than two minutes had come off the clock. Dubicki's point-after attempt went wide and the lead stood at 6-0.

The Boilermaker defense continued to dominate, repeatedly batting down passes and stopping Camp Grant runners for little or no gain. Joe Buscemi and Sam Vacanti each notched an interception in the second quarter. Unfortunately, the Boilermakers hadn't quite fixed the fumbling problems from the Illinois game as they turned it over three times themselves in the first half. Finally, midway through the second quarter, the Purdue attack was able to keep control of the ball long enough for a second scoring drive. The Boilermakers took over near midfield after a Camp Grant punt. Halfback Lew Rose gained nine on first down and Butkovich plowed ahead for a two-yard gain to earn a new set of downs. That combination worked so well the first time they tried it again, picking up 11 more yards to the Warrior 24. Vacanti then hit Frank Bauman for a 12-yard gain on a button-hook. On the next snap, Tony appeared to crash over the goal-line but the Boilermaker celebration was halted after Butkovich was ruled down at the two. All that did was delay the inevitable as Touchdown Tony followed his buddies Genis and Agase into the end zone around the right end on the very next play. Dubicki's kick was good this time and the Boilermakers took a 13-0 lead.

Burnham inserted the second unit to close out the first half and they were every bit as successful as the starters on defense. When the halftime gun sounded, the Camp Grant offense had accumulated -1 yard of total offense to go with two interceptions, two blocked punts and a fumble.

Purdue received the second half kickoff and quickly went to work on offense, this time through the air. For the first time all season, assistant coach Cecil Isbell's passing attack seemed to really click as Vacanti opened the third quarter with a 14-yard pass to Bauman and a 29-yard throw to Buscemi. The offense stalled out deep in Warrior territory but Babe Dimancheff got the ball right back with the team's third interception of the game. Dimancheff then gained 12 yards around the left end and Butkovich lowered his head for a five-yard gain down to the Warrior 7-yard line. With all of the weapons at his disposal, Vacanti caught the defense off guard by calling his own number. DiFilippo blasted a hole through the middle of the defense and Vacanti covered seven yards on the quarterback sneak. He missed the extra point and the score stayed at 19-0.

Purdue's offense didn't do a whole lot the rest of the way, advancing deep into Camp Grant territory just twice more before running out of downs short of the end zone. Fortunately, the same could be said for the Warriors as the Purdue defense continued to dominate. Burnham pulled the starters early in the fourth quarter, then brought in the third string at the midway point.

Two former Boilermakers helped the Camp Grant squad put together one last attempt. John Andretich intercepted a pass deep in his own end and returned it out past the 20. Teammate Bill Burghardt then took advantage of having one more chance to play on the Ross-Ade turf with a sparkling 37-yard run out past midfield. It appeared to all in attendance that Burghardt was destined to get the visiting team on the scoreboard but Charlie Haag, an undersized reserve end from Evansville and one of the few civilians on the Boilermaker roster, tracked him down from behind for the tackle. Burghardt completed a pass to the 12-yard line as the final gun sounded and the shutout was preserved, a 19-0 win for the home team. It was the second time in the last three games the Boilermaker defense had held an opponent off the scoreboard.

Purdue's offense was the most balanced it had been all season long with 153 yards in the rushing game to go with 122 passing yards.

Quarterbacks Sam Vacanti and Blaine Hibler combined to complete 11 of 18 passing attempts. Butkovich led the way on the ground with 50 yards and a score.

Camp Grant's offensive numbers, meanwhile, were a bit misleading. They ended the day with 80 on the ground and 61 through the air for 141 yards of total offense. But 64 of those yards came on that final drive against the Boilermaker third string defense. They completed just 5 of 17 through the air with three interceptions. Burghardt was the bright spot, rushing for 41 yards and throwing for 50, all in second half action.

The biggest question coming out of the game was just how good this Purdue team could be. With four dominant wins, including three over military installation squads, there were considerable rumblings that the front seven was the best in the country. A longtime newspaper man at the *Lafayette Journal & Courier*, sports editor Gordon Graham, mused after the game that it may be the best front line Purdue ever had.

"We seriously doubt that a better forward wall ever stepped foot on the turf at Ross-Ade Stadium than the one which operated for Purdue here Saturday afternoon," Graham wrote that evening following the game. "The play up front was so consistently spectacular that for once the average fan in the stands was watching and talking about the linemen even more than the backs...it's quite likely no conference team has ever had a better pair of guards than Agase and Barwegen."[8]

When the new AP Poll came out a few days after the win the Boilermakers had climbed to No. 5 in the country, their highest ranking in the history of the poll. Notre Dame put a stranglehold on the top spot with a dominant win over then-No.4 Michigan. Army was ranked second, Navy ranked third and Pennsylvania was in the No. 4 spot just ahead of the Boilermakers.[9]

As impressive as the win was over Camp Grant, it came at a cost. Starting left halfback and placekicker Stan Dubicki was lost, possibly for the season. The Marine transfer from Shurtleff College suffered a knee injury in the third quarter. It was a similar injury to the one that took down backfield mate Ed Cycenas during training camp. The South Bend, Ind., native was second on the team in scoring with three touchdowns, nine PATs and a field goal to his credit on the season. As the Boilermakers turned their attention to a road game against defending national champion Ohio State, they now had to figure out how to replace Dubicki and DiFilippo, two key components in their offensive juggernaut.

Soldiers walk on campus in 1942 as Purdue University quickly switched from a civilian institution to one with a strong military influence following the attack on Pearl Harbor. *(Photo credit: 1943 Purdue Debris, Purdue Athletics Archives)*

TOP - Intramural fields on campus were turned into parade grounds for U.S. Navy trainees. BOTTOM - Sailors await a train at the Big Four station in Lafayette, Ind. *(Photo credit: 1943 Purdue Debris, Purdue Athletics Archives)*

Commander Hugh J. Bartley oversaw the United States Naval Training Station at Purdue. *(Photo credit: 1943 Purdue Debris, Purdue Athletics)*

Cory Palm

DONALD LEHMKUHL
GUARD

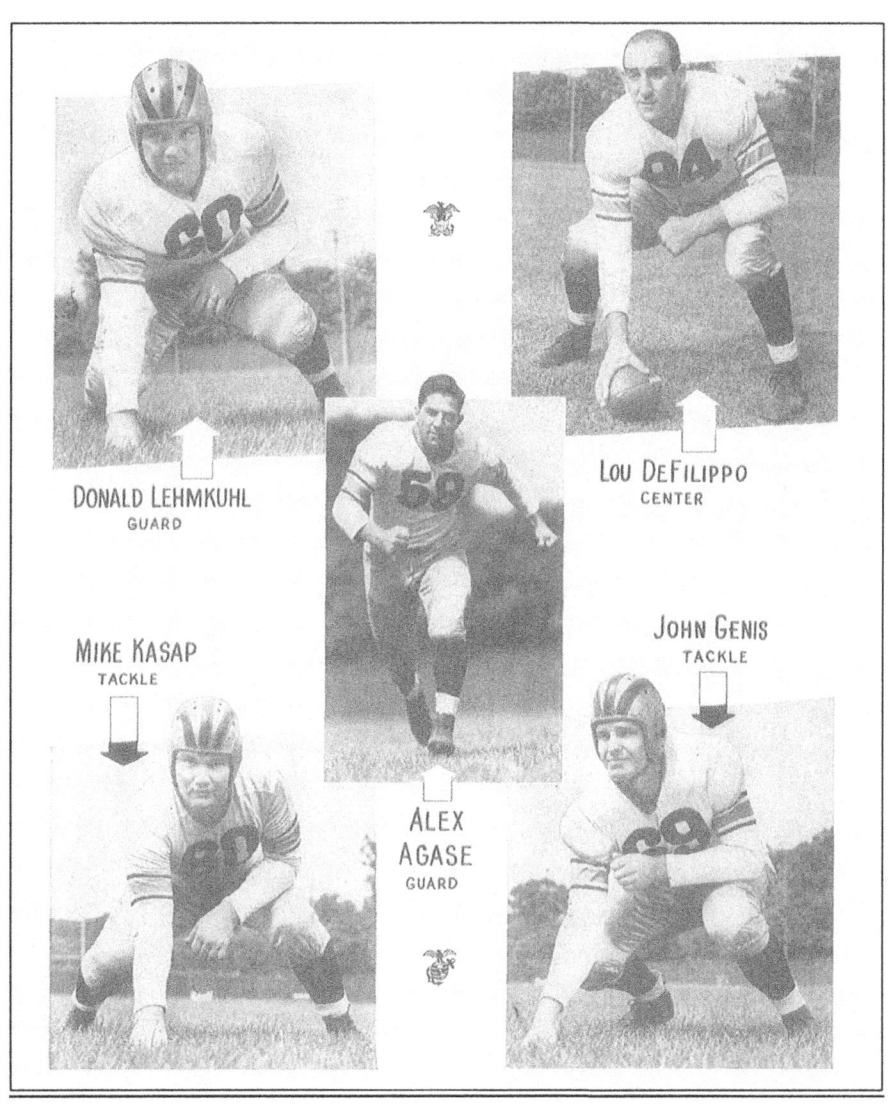

LOU DEFILIPPO
CENTER

MIKE KASAP
TACKLE

ALEX AGASE
GUARD

JOHN GENIS
TACKLE

ABOVE: The collection of talent on the offensive line was, by all accounts, amongst the best in school history. *(Photo credit: Purdue Athletics Archives)*
OPPOSITE PAGE: Top – The Purdue coaching wasn't complete until the summer of 1943. It included (left to right) Cecil Isbell, head coach Elmer Burnham, Joe Dienhart and Sam Voinoff. Bottom Right – Isbell led the NFL in passing in 1942 while with the Green Bay Packers before walking away to coach at his alma mater. Bottom Left – Burnham was in his second year as the head coach with the Boilermakers in 1943. *(Photo credit: Purdue Athletics Archives)*

The coaching staff spent all of preseason and the first several weeks trying to determine the best combination of talent for the backfield. The only thing they knew for certain was that Tony Butkovich would be their fullback. *(Photo credit: Purdue Athletics Archives)*

ABOVE: Boris "Babe" Dimancheff transferred in just before the season began. By season's end, he was the best halfback on the squad. BELOW: Dick Barwegen was a rarity in 1943: a civilian with previous experience at Purdue. *(Photo credit: Purdue Athletics Archives)*

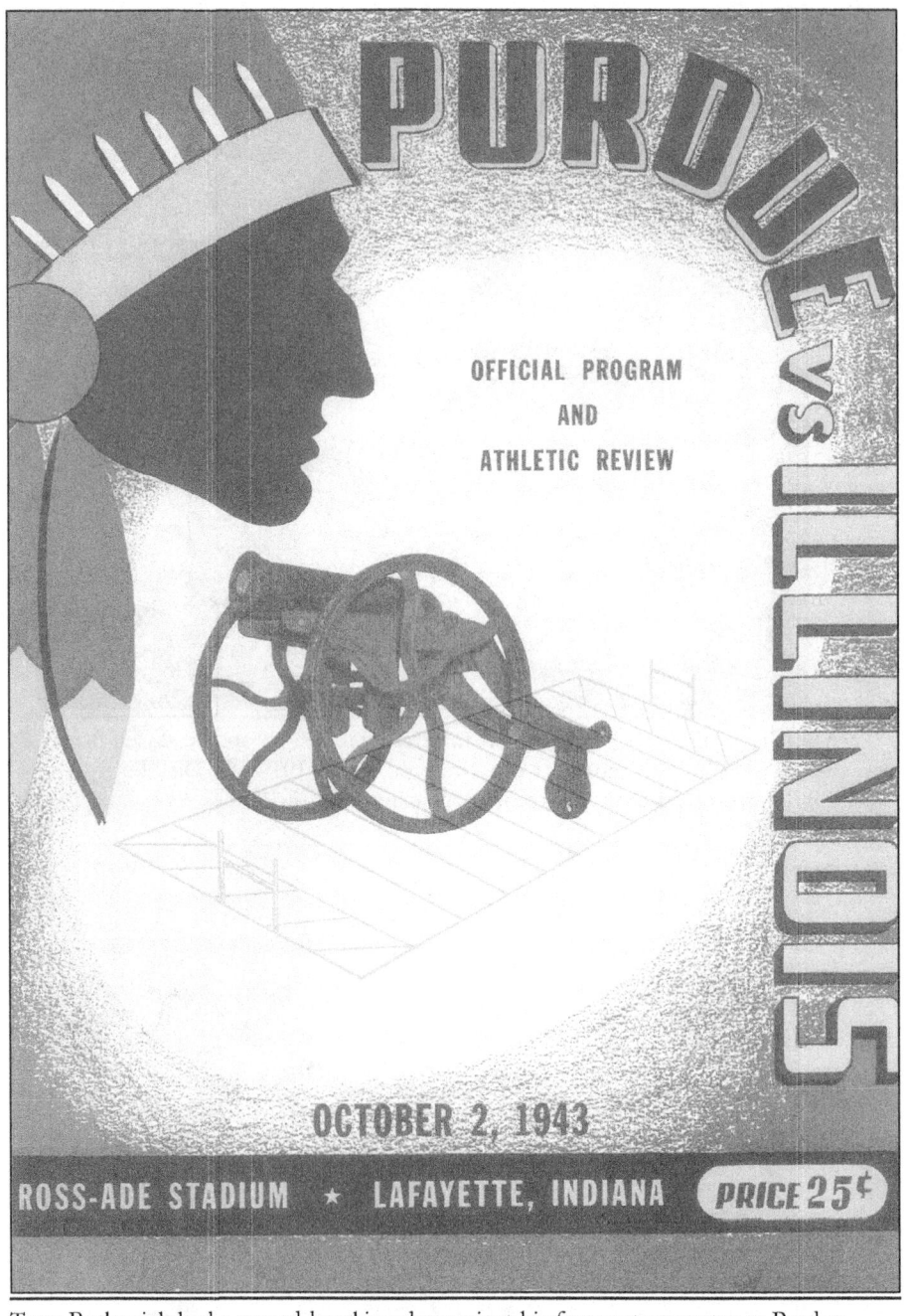

Tony Butkovich had a record-breaking day against his former teammates as Purdue and Illinois renewed their rivalry, with a new trophy, in Week Three. (*Photo Courtesy: Purdue Athletics Archive*)

Week Four featured a dominant win over the soldiers from Camp Grant, 28-7. *(Photo credit: Purdue Athletics Archives)*

A big fourth quarter sparked the Homecoming win over Iowa as rumors of Navy transfers dominated the week on campus. *(Photo credit: Purdue Athletics Archives)*

The Boilermakers closed out the perfect season with a thrilling win over Indiana. Multiple red zone stops in the fourth quarter allowed Purdue to capture the Old Oaken Bucket and finish 9-0. *(Photo credit: Purdue Athletics Archives)*

Cory Palm

TOP: Tony Butkovich finds an opening against Great Lakes with Mike Kasap (64) and Joe Buscemi (50) leading the way. *(Photo credit: Purdue Athletics Archives)*
BOTTOM: Alex Agase (front row, third from right) and Tony Butkovich (back row, second from right) were part of Uncle Sam's All-Star Team while on Parris Island. *(Photo credit: National Archives and Records Administration)*

Perfect Warriors

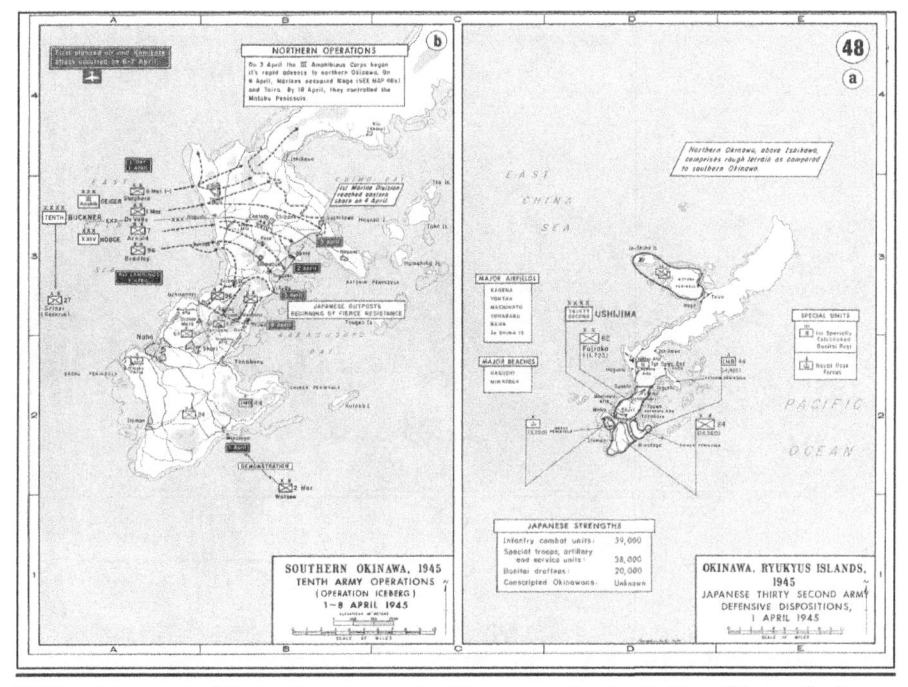

TOP: Map of Allied Invasion of Okinawa, April 1945. (*Photo Credit: HistoricalResrouces.Wordpress.com*)
BOTTOM: Allied troops come ashore in Okinawa, April 1945. (*Photo Credit: National Archives*)

TOP: Marines from the 6th marine division engage in the battle for Yae-Take, the engagement that saw Corporal Tony Butkovich fall victim to a sniper bullet. *(Source: U.S. Army)*

BOTTOM: More than a dozen members from the 1943 Purdue team gathered in Ross-Ade Stadium on the 40th Anniversary of their historic season. *(Photo credit: Purdue Athletics Archives)*

Perfect Warriors

Row 1 (R to L) – Leo Milla, Stanley Dubicki, Gilbert Mordoh, Boris Dimancheff, Joe Buscemi, Frank Bauman, Dick Barwegen, Joseph Hersch, Don Lehmkuhl. Row 2 – George Mihal, Tom Hughes, William O. Keefe, Bill Stuart, Alex Agase, Tony Butkovich, John Genis, Blaine Hibler, Ed Gerker, Keith Parker, Ed Cycenas Row 3 – Dick Butsch (Manager), Dick Bushnell, Chalmers "Bump" Elliott, Joe Morrow, Charlie Haag, Wells Ellis, Herb Hoffman, James Darr, James McMillen, Sam Vacanti, Lou DeFilippo Row 4 – Williams Newell, James Lockwood, Nathan Laskin, Walt Poremba, Stan Schultz, John Staak, Jack Butt, Arthur Flint, James Laughter, Mike Kasap. (Photo Credit: Purdue Athletics Archive)

CHAPTER 11

| WEEK FIVE |
VS. OHIO STATE IN CLEVELAND

The game of football was certainly affected by the war in 1943 at all levels. There was a lack of manpower due to the draft as well as financial shortfalls and travel restrictions that affected college and professional teams rather dramatically. Hundreds of colleges suspended their football programs and two NFL teams were forced to merge their operations in order to remain viable. But, of course, football wasn't the only sport affected.

Major League Baseball was drastically changed by the war as well. More than 500 active major leaguers served overseas, including legends of the sport like Ted Williams, Joe DiMaggio, Stan Musial and Bob Feller.[1] Travel restrictions affected scheduling and wartime blackout restrictions seriously limited night games. Another area of the sport affected was the annual ritual of spring training for the teams. MLB Commissioner Kennesaw Mountain Landis worked with the Office of

Defense Transportation to find a sensible solution to the need for spring training.[2]

Because train lines were busy transporting troops and supplies around the country and there was rationing on everything from food to fuel, a compromise was reached. Major League teams were mandated that they could not go south. In fact, they would have to find training locations north of the Ohio and Potomac Rivers and east of the Mississippi.[3] That decision led to a more regionalized approach for teams. In early 1943, the Brooklyn Dodgers trained at West Point, N.Y., and the Washington Senators found a temporary home at the University of Maryland. The New York Yankees headed to the Jersey Shore resort town of Asbury Park and the Cleveland Indians found their spring training home at Purdue.[4]

For Indians General Manager Roger Peckinpaugh, the choice to spend the early spring in West Lafayette was an easy one, not because of its climate but because of the recently constructed Purdue Fieldhouse. Completed in 1937, the Fieldhouse was the central hub for Purdue Athletics. For Peckinpaugh, it was the perfect home away from home.

"It has an earth floor large enough to lay out a football field," he said. "And we could hold infield practice there as readily as outdoors. It's the last word in fieldhouses."[5]

Indians player-manager Lou Boudreau and his squad arrived in mid-March and got right to work. The future American League MVP actually arrived a few days early and went through the facilities with athletics director Red Mackey. Boudreau was already well acquainted with Purdue and the Fieldhouse. The Indians shortstop actually played baseball and basketball at the University of Illinois and during his final season in Champaign, in which he was named an All-American on the hardwood, he had played basketball in the fieldhouse during its inaugural season.[6]

Boudreau led the Indians in daily drills in the fieldhouse from 10 each morning until 1 each afternoon, heading to the outdoor fields whenever the weather would permit. Batting cages were hung in the fieldhouse and an infield was designed, allowing for a good approximation of real conditions. The team even had the chance to scrimmage against the Purdue baseball team on occasion, including on their final day on campus. During those practice games, the Cleveland squad furnished the pitching and catching for both sides but the

Boilermakers got to play against the major leaguers. More than a thousand fans turned out for the final scrimmage between the squads in early April.[7]

After a little more than three weeks on campus, Boudreau and his team headed back to Cleveland but not before roundly praising all aspects of the situation at Purdue. In fact, the team enjoyed their stay so much it became their home for the duration of the war as the Tribe returned to campus in March 1944 and 1945. Thanks to an interesting bit of scheduling happenstance, the Indians had a chance in the fall of 1943 to return the favor of good hospitality.

Ohio State had taken to playing one home game in Cleveland during WWII, despite the nearly 150 miles separating the city from campus. In 1942 and 1944, they hosted Illinois in Cleveland Stadium. For the 1943 season, they would welcome Purdue to the field the Indians called home.[8]

That 1942 version of the Ohio State football team was an absolute juggernaut. Ranked as the No. 1 team for the first six weeks of the season, they reeled off five straight dominant wins to start the season, including a 26-0 demolishing of Purdue at Ohio Stadium in Columbus. The Buckeyes lost in week six to sixth-ranked Wisconsin in Madison, then won their final four games to finish 9-1. Ohio State caught a break when Wisconsin slipped up against an unranked Iowa squad and finished the season 8-1-1, after an early-season tie with Notre Dame.[9]

The Buckeyes had late-season wins against a top-15 Illinois squad and a fourth-ranked Michigan team and when the season was over, second-year head coach Paul Brown earned his only college national title as the Associated Press conferred the top spot on the Scarlett and Grey. Five members from that squad earned All-America honors, the most of any team in the country. And the team in 1943? Well, the team in 1943 didn't resemble that squad one little bit.

Ohio State University was not selected as a member of the Navy's V-12 program. It was the home to more than 600 military personnel in the Army Specialized Training Program but once again the decision by the War Department to not allow Army trainees to take part in intercollegiate athletics reared its head. As the 1943 campaign began, Coach Brown found himself with just seven returning letter-winners and a whole bunch of fresh faces, mostly 17-year-old freshmen ineligible for the draft as of yet.[10]

With such a young squad and a tough schedule, the Buckeyes were 1-2 on the year with a win over Missouri sandwiched between losses to Iowa Pre-Flight and Great Lakes. Their 13-6 loss at Great Lakes the previous week suggested that things were improving. Ohio State held the sailors scoreless in the first half and responded to Great Lakes' first score with six points of their own in the third quarter. But the Buckeyes wore down late, giving up a touchdown deep in the fourth quarter as the Bluejackets pulled away. Freshman halfback Dean Sensanbaugher seemed a star in the making for Ohio State and he electrified the crowd with a 97-yard kickoff return in the second half but the Buckeye offense managed just 110 yards on the day. They'd be in for a long day against Purdue if the attack didn't improve.

As for the Boilermakers, their game week preparation was of a different sort. Head Coach Elmer Burnham, the newly minted United Press National Coach of the Week, used Monday's workout to switch things up. No helmets or shoulder pads were allowed. Linemen found themselves taking handoffs in the backfield and the running backs were up front, hands in the dirt, and figuring out blocking schemes as the team laughed and joked through an hour of touch football inside the confines of Ross-Ade Stadium.[11]

"These boys are playing football for fun all the time and that's the way it should be played," Burnham said after the workout. "We don't take ourselves or anyone else too seriously."[12]

It wasn't that Burnham was taking the Buckeyes lightly. He knew they were a young but improving squad and that Paul Brown was a rising star as a head coach. Legendary Purdue basketball coach Ward "Piggy" Lambert had actually taken on the job of scouting the Buckeyes in their game against Great Lakes. He reported back that Ohio State had a pair of halfbacks of particular note. The first was Sensanbaugher, who got everyone's attention with the long kickoff return against the Bluejackets. The second was fellow freshman Ernie Parks. The youngster had run for 186 yards and three touchdowns against Missouri, just his second college game, and possessed sprinter speed, having been an Ohio state champion in the 100-yard and the 220-yard sprints in high school.[13]

But Parks, one of two African-Americans in the Buckeye starting lineup along with the outstanding lineman Bill Willis, was already on borrowed time. On Oct. 8, just a little over a week before the Purdue game, Parks had sworn an oath to the U.S. Army, joining the Enlisted

Reserve Corps.[14] He would be activated soon and was hoping to remain on campus through the end of the football season. He would, in fact, do just that before getting his orders in early January. But on this mid-October afternoon in Cleveland, he and Sensanbaugher would likely be a problem for the Boilermakers.

The Boilermakers went through their final heavy practice on Thursday afternoon and did a light workout early Friday before boarding their Big Four train at around 4:30 Friday afternoon. After a solid seven hours of riding the rails, they arrived at the Cleveland Union Terminal station just before midnight. The travel squad included 36 players, although at least two of them would not see the field as Ed Cycenas was still out and Stan Dubicki was only a possible participant exclusively for his kicking duties. Bill Stuart would get the start in place of Dubicki at the left halfback spot and center Lou DiFilippo would be replaced by Joe Morrow, a Marine transfer from Missouri who had played extensively but was making his first start for the Boilermakers.

And if the scouting reports weren't enough of a motivating factor for the Boilermakers, several players had the unique collective memory of losing results from the 1942 season. The Purdue coaching staff and the handful of roster holdovers from the previous season couldn't shake the memory of Ohio State's 26-0 shutout in Columbus. And the several former Illinois players on the squad were eager to avenge the 44-20 loss at the hands of the Buckeyes the previous November right there in Cleveland Stadium. Heck, fullback Leo Milla may have still been holding a grudge from the 1941 season when his Missouri Tigers opened the season with a loss to the Buckeyes, though Milla would not be making the trip to Cleveland with the travel squad.

The Boilermakers would be playing in front of the largest crowd they would see all season as nearly 42,000 fans came through the turnstiles of Cleveland Stadium, including a large contingent of Purdue alumni from northeast Ohio, although steady rain and a brisk wind off of Lake Erie on gameday actually kept the crowd down from an expected total of more than 60,000. What's more, the game had garnered national attention with NBC Radio broadcasting the contest along with seven different independent regional stations.

And all of those in attendance and listening at home were witnesses to a sloppy and surprising first half. Purdue received the kickoff to start to game and a long run by Babe Dimancheff seemed to set a good tone. But Sam Vacanti fumbled near midfield and Ohio State recovered. The Purdue defense stood tall, forcing a punt but a good kick and a clipping penalty pinned the Boilermakers deep. On the first play of the ensuing drive, Tony Butkovich put the ball on the ground and once again the Buckeyes recovered, this time at the Boilermaker 6-yard line. Sensanbaugher took a pitch wide right and trotted into the end zone, giving the Buckeyes a 7-0 lead before they had even gained a first down.

For the rest of the half the Boilermakers dominated the run of play but could never quite close the deal. As the game reached intermission, Ohio State had gained just one first down to Purdue's 11 in the half. The Boilermakers dominated time of possession and total yards but also had turned it over in key times and had seen untimely penalties snuff out a few scoring threats. To make matters even more tenuous, the rain continued and the field conditions got worse with every passing minute.

In the locker room, the Purdue coaching staff huddled and discussed how to combat the surprising Ohio State defensive alignment. The Buckeyes had rolled out a six-man defensive front with an extra linebacker and two defensive backs. Purdue had experimented with a five-man defensive front early in the season to give a couple extra linebackers to stymie the opposing offense so they knew a bit about the vulnerabilities of the modified defensive front. Now the hope was that some blocking scheme adjustments would allow the offensive line to reach the second level of the defense and create a bit more space. The team was so eager to get back out to the playing field and right the wrongs of the first half that not a single man took a seat in the locker room during the intermission.

Ohio State got the second half kick and gained their second first down of the day before being forced to punt, the Boilermakers taking over at their own 18-yard line. Then a surprise hero stood up for the Boilermakers. Keith Parker, the Marine transfer from Missouri, trotted onto the field at right halfback. Parker had spent most of the season with the third string but injuries had provided him an opportunity that he was determined to make the most of.

A Butkovich run gained four on the first play and on second down, Parker took a hand-off between Agase and Genis on the right side of the line for 16 yards. Butkovich fumbled on the next play but Mike

Kasap recovered for Purdue as the offense finally caught a break. Then Parker took another handoff and shot through a hole in the center of the line and looked destined to get the Boilermakers on the board. Ernie Parks put his sprinting skills to use and was able to run down Parker but not before a 46-yard gain down to the Ohio State 8-yard line. Three plays later Butkovich crashed over the goal line but Dubicki missed the PAT and the Buckeyes clung to a 7-6 lead.

Purdue's defense forced a quick three-and-out and the offense went to work once more. Keeping things as simple as possible as the conditions deteriorated, the Boilermakers covered all 48 yards on the ground in the course of 11 plays, Butkovich again gaining the final two yards and scoring his second touchdown of the day. Another missed PAT kept the score 12-7 in favor of Purdue. Just before the end of the third quarter, Sensanbaugher fumbled and Agase recovered. The Boilermakers began the fourth quarter with the ball once again deep in Buckeye territory but a 15-yard penalty stalled out the drive and Ohio State took back over. It would be the only drive of the second half Purdue did not result in points for the Boilermakers.

Parks lost another fumble for the Buckeyes on the next snap and Butkovich soon crashed over the goal line for his third score and an 18-7 lead. Another Ohio State punt led to another sustained Purdue drive as the holes in the center of the defense continued to grow, the vaunted Boilermaker front line exerting its dominance. Babe Dimancheff covered the final 33 yards on the drive after taking a handoff and scampering across the goal line.

Ohio State went nowhere on its next possession and on fourth down Dick Barwegen burst through the line and blocked the punt, giving his offense the ball at the Buckeye 30. Six plays later, Dimancheff took a toss wide left and followed a wall of blockers for a 15-yard score and the Boilermakers closed it out 30-7 with all five tallies coming in the dominant second half.

It was maybe the finest defensive performance of the season for Purdue as they surrendered just 76 total yards to Ohio State, including zero yards through the air. The Buckeyes only earned three first downs in the game to Purdue's 21 and the Buckeyes were forced to punt 10 times.

The Boilermaker offense reaped the rewards of those halftime adjustments by Burnham and his staff. Butkovich finished the game with 36 carries for 123 yards and three scores while Dimancheff carried 16 times for 122 yards and two touchdowns. When Dimancheff wasn't in the game at right halfback his running mate Parker made the most of his three carries from the spot, going 57 yards while being the force that broke the dam early in the second half. The Boilermaker run game finished with 350 yards on 70 carries, more than double the rushing attempts Ohio State had on the afternoon.

In the locker room after the game, with the tension of a stressful afternoon finally relieved, the team was ready for some light conversation. It came in the telling of a pretty nerve-wracking situation just before kickoff. Reserve halfback Dick Bushnell and tackle Tom Hughes, who would handle the kickoff duties for the day with Dubicki injured, got separated from the team and couldn't gain entry to the stadium. "I've got to kick off in a few minutes," exclaimed Hughes, trying to talk his way through the gate.[15]

Hughes finally pulled out his Marine Corps identification card and had the usher compare the picture to the one in the game program. Finally, the gatekeeper believed Bushnell and Hughes and agreed to let them pass, but not before looking at the civilian running back and telling him he looked too young and too small to be a football player. All's well that ends well, as Hughes and Bushnell made it to the dressing room in time to join the team for the game. They shared a good laugh and made their way to the train station to settle in for a happy seven-hour ride home. The Boilermakers had vanquished another Big Ten foe, gained some measure of revenge and improved to 5-0. As the train rushed into darkness, all was right in their little corner of the world.

CHAPTER 12

| WEEK SIX |
VS. IOWA

With the win over Ohio State, Purdue had risen to No. 4 in the country, trailing Notre Dame, Army and Navy in the latest AP Poll. The Fighting Irish had demolished Wisconsin 51-0 to retain the top spot. Army dominated Columbia 52-0 for the second spot and Navy got by Penn State by a 14-6 score to hold onto third. The Boilermakers' win at Ohio State was impressive enough to leapfrog Penn despite the Quakers running up a 74-6 win on Lakehurst Naval Air Station.[1]

Purdue turned its attention to an Iowa squad that had been decimated by the war. The Hawkeyes had a respectable 6-4 record in 1942, which included a win over second-ranked Wisconsin late in the year. Head coach Eddie Anderson, in his fourth year with the club, was one of the most fascinating figures in all of college football.

*   *   *   *   *

Anderson began his tenure in Iowa City in 1939 by mentoring the great Nile Kinnick to the Heisman Trophy and the Hawkeyes to 6-1-1 record and a Top Ten ranking.[2]

By his fourth season, Anderson had compiled a 19-14-1 record with the Hawkeyes while spending a significant amount of time across the way at the University Hospital. You see, Dr. Eddie Anderson really began his football coaching career as a means to pay for medical school. After playing for Knute Rockne at Notre Dame, where he earned All-America honors his senior year, Anderson slid into coaching. He spent two seasons with Columbia College in Dubuque, Iowa, before taking a player/coach role with the Chicago Cardinals in the NFL.

While in Chicago, first with the Cardinals then as the head coach at DePaul University, Anderson enrolled at Rush Medical College. Upon graduating from Rush, Dr. Anderson took the head football coaching position at Holy Cross in Massachusetts. While leading the Crusaders to great success on the field, Anderson also practiced medicine at Veteran's Hospital in Boston. Anderson continued that regimen after taking the job in Iowa City, spending his mornings at University Hospital before heading to the football offices and the practice field each afternoon.[3]

In February 1943, after months of internal struggle about wanting to take a more active role in the war effort, Anderson resigned his position at the University of Iowa and was sworn in as a Major in the Army Medical Corps. Athletics director E.G. Schroeder publicly declared that the door would be open for Anderson to return at the conclusion of the war, which is exactly what would happen. Anderson returned in 1946 and coached the Hawkeyes for four more seasons before closing out his career back at Holy Cross. By the time he retired in 1964, he had compiled over 200 wins in his coaching career.

* * * * *

But in the moment, with Anderson suddenly gone, the Hawkeyes were seven months away from the start of the season and had to figure out not only their personnel on the field but also who would lead them.

To make matters worse, Iowa was not selected by the Navy as a participant in the V-12 program and, as such, saw key players shipped off to other locations. That included Purdue starting quarterback Sam

Vacanti, a talented athlete who had already earned letters in football, basketball and baseball for the Hawkeyes. Adding further insult to the situation was the fact that, in 1942, the Navy established the Iowa Pre-Flight School on campus in Iowa City. Iowa Pre-Flight would use university resources but was established as separate from the university itself and, as such, would compete as a separate entity on the gridiron. The Iowa Pre-Flight Seahawks played in the same stadium, studied in the same classrooms and walked the same quad as the civilian Hawkeyes. But when it came time to compete, the Seahawks and the Hawkeyes were completely separate.[4]

Like most of the other military installations competing around the nation, the Seahawks were only active from 1942-44 but they averaged nearly nine wins a year in that span and twice finished ranked in the Top Ten in the country, including wrapping the 1943 season as the No. 2 team in the land. The Hawkeyes, meanwhile, were scrambling just to get a team together.

The year didn't get any better for Iowa supporters in early June when word came that the greatest Hawkeye of all was gone, suddenly and tragically. In 1940, Nile Kinnick had turned down offers to play professional football in favor of enrolling at the university's law school. A year later, he decided to join the Navy Air Reserves and was inducted three days before the Japanese attack on Pearl Harbor. Training to be a fighter pilot, Kinnick was deployed on the *USS Lexington* in May 1943. On June 2, Kinnick died whilst on a training mission off the coast of Venezuela. Hawkeye hearts were heavy at the loss of their legend. When news broke back home a few days later, the headline and accompanying articles and photo in *The Daily Iowan* took up half of the front page, along with a letter from the editor that took up most of page two and most of the sports page.[5] It was the ultimate blow in what was shaping up to be a terrible year, indeed, for Iowa football.

On the gridiron, interim head coach Edward "Slip" Madigan was eventually picked to succeed Anderson and arrived on campus in early July.[6] By September, Madigan had a roster of 57 players, more than half of whom had missed the summer drills allowed by the NCAA because they were incoming freshmen. The youth and inexperience showed on the field as the Hawkeyes began the season with losses to Great Lakes, Wisconsin and Iowa Pre-Flight before tying Indiana 7-7.

That tie against the Hoosiers was as good as a victory for the Hawks as they throttled what was the nation's best passing attack in the effort. Iowa held the Hoosiers to just 128 yards of total offense. In fact, Iowa shut out the Indiana offense as the only points the Hoosiers scored were on an interception returned for a touchdown. But Iowa didn't have much time to enjoy that positive result. Now they had to gear up for one of the nation's most formidable rushing attacks. Through five games, the Boilermakers were averaging 5.2 yards per carry as a team and had gained over 1,200 yards rushing on the season, an average of 252 yards per game. The 35-man Hawkeye travel squad hit the rails Friday afternoon, bound for Chicago. After a night at the Morrison Hotel, they rode down to Lafayette, scheduled to arrive a little less than two hours before kickoff. And the Boilermaker team that would be waiting for them? Well, it was a bit distracted.

It was homecoming week on campus and there were plenty of the requisite activities that go along with that yearly celebration. The fall session was wrapping up, with students all across campus, football players included, preparing for final exams. In addition, some controversy was stirred when the Boilermakers were featured prominently in a cartoon on the front page of the Oct. 17, 1943 Sunday Edition of the *Chicago Tribune*. The drawing took up three columns worth of space above the fold with the headline reading "'Purdue et al' is making a grand record; Purdue says: 'War is helpful'." The first frame featured eleven football players with Purdue P's on their chest, all yelling "Bully for old Purdue! – Whee!!". However, in the second slide, the players turned around and revealed various school logos from their original institutions of Illinois, Fordham, Iowa, Missouri and Shurtleff.[7]

The cartoon seemed to be taking a swipe at the mercenary nature of the Boilermakers' success. Local publications responded to those accusations by pointing out that the cartoonist was none other than the famed Purdue alumnus John T. McCutcheon. The Pulitzer Prize-winning cartoonist was the staff illustrator for the Tribune for more than four decades, his political cartoons often appearing on the front page. An 1889 graduate of Purdue, McCutcheon worked at the student newspaper, *The Purdue Exponent,* while on campus and was also editor of the school's first yearbook. He was a major supporter of his alma mater and its athletic teams throughout the years. As such, his two former employers in his home town found it unlikely that McCutcheon was taking a shot at his beloved Purdue.

Still, Gordon Graham, the sports editor for the *Lafayette Journal & Courier*, felt compelled to write a column defending the team and the university. "The present Boilermaker squad is composed of as fine a group of young men as we ever saw in Purdue uniforms," Graham wrote. "We know that all other football schools would play these men and that Purdue is living up to the rules of the Big Ten by playing them."[8]

Whatever the motivation of the illustrator, the fact remained that the Purdue Football team had risen to the level of prominence where it was given significant space on the front page of one of the nation's most important newspapers. It was publicity that the university couldn't buy if it wanted to and proof that the football team was on a national stage, indeed.

Monday practice, as had become the custom, was very light for the Boilermakers. They spent most of the session studying scouting reports of the Hawkeyes and getting details from assistant coach Sam Voinoff who had gone to watch Iowa play Indiana. The extra rest also helped several players heal after the rough and tumble game in Cleveland. The backfield was particularly affected with halfbacks Stan Dubicki, Keith Parker, Bill Stuart and Babe Dimancheff all nursing injuries along with starting ends Joe Buscemi and Frank Bauman.

As gameday approached, it seemed clear that Bauman would be out along with Stewart and Parker. Backup right end Bill O'Keefe would take Bauman's place, as he had done late in the game in Cleveland. And the backfield would be bolstered by the return of Lew Rose, the talented sophomore who had played sparingly due to the wealth of talented runners in Coach Burnham's stable. Dubicki and Dimancheff appeared ready to go as well.

Aside from a controversial cartoon, a whole heap of injuries and the pomp and circumstance of a homecoming game against a conference rival, a different circumstance kept Boilermakers occupied throughout the week. Rumors had begun to spread around campus that the first round of Navy V-12 deployments were imminent. Other universities had already received word that officer trainees were being activated. Notre Dame, Michigan, Northwestern and Marquette all announced that their teams were taking a hit as the Navy activated members of their training programs.[9, 10] Closer to home, having been ruled out of the Iowa game due to injuries, Ed Cycenas and Bill Stuart were ordered to report on October 30 after a week-long furlough. Both would then be transferred from campus to their next training station.[11]

This day had been on the horizon from the moment the V-12 trainees stepped on campus, an ever-present, often unspoken of, reality that grew nearer each minute. But now, with the fall term coming to a close and the decision looming, there were more questions than answers. When would official word come for the bulk of the V-12 trainees on the team? What date would they be ordered to ship out? How would these decisions affect the remaining four games of the season? Would the team be able to maintain focus versus Iowa with the future up in the air? Could this game against the Hawkeyes be the final game with the full Boilermaker squad?

Purdue opened the game like a team struggling to maintain focus. More than 15,000 fans packed into Ross-Ade Stadium for the homecoming contest. They saw the visiting team take an early lead and control the game for most of the first half. The Hawkeyes received the opening kick and went three-and-out, punting the ball over to the Boilermakers. On their first offensive snap, Butkovich rumbled for 20 yards before fumbling. The Hawkeyes recovered on the Purdue 44-yard line. Iowa varied their play calling, sprinkling in a few successful pass plays to go with some solid inside running and when Paul Glasener sprinted around the end for a 19-yard touchdown run, the Hawks had stunned the home crowd.

The road team carried that lead into the second quarter when Touchdown Tony was finally able to atone for his early mistake. Taking the ball at midfield following an Iowa punt, the Boilermakers ran on nine consecutive plays with Butkovich finishing the drive off with an 8-yard sweep straight into the end zone. Just four minutes into the second quarter the Boilermakers had tied the game at 7-7. That's where the score stayed until the break.

During intermission, after the two squads had retired to their locker rooms to make adjustments to set about solving the questions asked in the first 30 minutes, a special ceremony was held on the field. The 1918 Purdue team was honored, commemorating the 25th anniversary of their very unique season in West Lafayette. That season, first-year coach Butch Scanlon's squad notched a 3-3 record overall but took down the University of Chicago in the season's only conference game to finish 1-0 and earn a share of the Big Ten title, the first in program history. It was one of the strangest years in college football history. With the United States ramping up military efforts after entering WWI, the Selective Service Act of 1917 had led to a major shortage of college-aged men to field teams, much like issues facing colleges across America a quarter-century later.

Making matters worse in 1918 was the Spanish Flu pandemic, which affected young adults at a disproportionate rate. This double whammy led many schools and some entire conferences to cancel the 1918 season. But the Boilermakers persevered. Several members from that squad made their way onto the field at halftime to receive an ovation from the crowd and silver football trophies from the Purdue Alumni Association.[12]

When the current team returned to the field to begin the second half, little had changed from the lackluster end to the first 30 minutes. The Boilermakers got the ball to begin the third quarter and after driving deep into Iowa territory, Butkovich once again fumbled away a chance to score. This time Tony had broken through the line and seemed destined to put his team on top when he dropped the ball and Iowa recovered at the 17-yard line. The defense stood tall, forcing a quick Iowa punt but the Hawkeyes retained possession after Purdue was called for roughing the punter. The teams traded punts for the rest of the quarter and headed to the final frame still knotted at 7-7.

The Hawkeyes had the ball and a bit of momentum after intercepting Vacanti in the closing seconds of the third quarter but once again the Boilermaker defense answered the bell and forced a punt. Purdue's offense come back onto the field, 71-yards away from the goal line and with just 12 minutes remaining in the contest. No doubt there were anxious moments in the stands as it had been weeks since the team had been pushed this deep into a game with the outcome still in doubt. Sure, they trailed at the half the prior Saturday in Cleveland but had made quick work of the Buckeyes in the second half. Well, fortunes can change quickly when you have the nation's best fullback.

On the first play of the ensuing drive, Butkovich ran a sweep around the right end for a 38-yard gain as the home crowd's anxiety was released all at once, 15,000 fans leaping to their feet in exultation. Dimancheff gained three on the next play and on second-and-7, Vacanti decided to try the other flank. He tossed a lateral to Butkovich around the left end and Touchdown Tony followed a wall of blockers all the way to pay dirt, breaking two Iowa tackles in the final five yards to close the deal. Three plays, 71 yards and a lead the Boilermakers would not relinquish.

Perhaps still stunned by the speed of the Boilermakers' decisive blow, the ensuing kickoff was an abject disaster for the Hawkeyes. Tom Hughes kicked off and as the ball bounced around the Ross-Ade turf, several Iowa players just stood and watched. Hustling down field to try to make a tackle, Joe Buscemi instead found himself covering a live ball and the Boilermaker offense once again took the field, this time at the Iowa 26. Butkovich and Dimancheff again split ball carrying duties with Tony scoring his third touchdown of the day on a six-yard plunge up the middle. That made the score 21-7 in favor of the home team and called an end to the action for the Boilermaker starters.

The reserves added a fourth score for good measure when the Purdue defense pushed Iowa deep into their own territory and then watched a snap sail over the Hawkeye quarterback's head into the end zone. Sophomore end Nathan Laskin recovered and put the cherry on top of the 28-7 final. To go with his three scores, Butkovich also led the rushing attack with 149 yards on 19 carries as the ground game gained 231 yards on the day.

More impressively, the Purdue defense stood tall with perhaps its best game of the season for the third week in a row. The Hawkeyes gained just 28 rushing yards despite running the ball 31 times on the afternoon. They also completed just four of 14 passes and threw two interceptions. Despite a shaky start and heading into the fourth quarter tied up, it ended up being a dominant performance for Purdue, improving the record to 6-0. On the national stage, everyone above the Boilermakers held serve. In what was believed to be their final game with star quarterback Angelo Bertelli, top-ranked Notre Dame defeated Illinois 47-0. Bertelli, who would be awarded the Heisman Trophy after the season, had already received orders from the Marines to report to Parris Island by Nov. 1. Second-ranked Army beat Yale 39-7 and third-ranked Navy took down Georgia Tech 28-14. The rankings remained the same when the latest AP Poll was released on the following Monday.[13]

But all of that took a back seat on Tuesday afternoon when the official word from the United States Navy finally reached West

Lafayette: the first wave of V-12 trainees were all ordered to report to campus on November 1 to ship out.[14] The squad would have one more game together, on October 30th at Wisconsin, before the first group of future officers would head off to a higher calling, to Parris Island and after that the Pacific Theatre to fight for the fate of the free world.

CHAPTER 13

| WEEK SEVEN |
AT WISCONSIN

When the official word came from Cmdr. Hugh J. Bartley, the officer presiding over Purdue's naval training school, it wasn't a surprise. After all, this day was the reason so many of the current Boilermakers even found themselves on campus to begin with. And, to a man, there was no loss of perspective of life's priorities. After all, as a column in the *Lafayette Journal & Courier* put it, they were in the Marines to be Marines.[1] Football was fun and their education was important but the opportunity to fight for something larger than themselves was a motivator for an entire generation of men. These men of Purdue were no different.

Twelve Boilermakers were involved in the first wave of call-ups and, while the number itself was large, the real issue was the identities of the dozen men that had been selected. The roll included starters Alex Agase, John Genis and Tony Butkovich along with key reserves Tom Hughes, John Staak, Jimmy Darr, Bill O'Keefe, Leo Milla and Bill "Pinky" Newell. Add in the departure the previous week of Ed Cycenas, Bill Stuart and Gilbert Murdoh and head coach Elmer Burnham suddenly found himself without a third of his 36 man travel roster.[2]

The nine transferring Marines gathered in Coach Burnham's office shortly after the announcement. The men were anxious and ready for the next step in their mission while also praising every aspect of their experience at Purdue.

"Two weekend leaves from Parris Island sure would be nice," joked Butkovich. "I'd sure like to help Purdue beat Minnesota and Indiana. But I'm thankful we got six games in. When do we leave?"[3]

Agase joined in the conversation with a challenge to his teammates remaining on campus.

"You guys staying around here had better win those last games," the once and future All-American guard said. "We are expecting to open a little package in about a month and if it doesn't contain those little gold footballs, there's going to be trouble."[4]

The Boilermakers, at 6-0 weren't just ranked 4th in the nation. They were also tied atop the Big Ten standings with a top-ten Michigan squad whose only loss had come out of conference against Notre Dame. Closing out the season undefeated would guarantee the Big Ten title that Agase was referring to. It would be Purdue's first conference crown in over a decade and the first perfect season since 1929. And, sure, winning was a priority for Coach Burnham. But the man who had always stressed the importance of finding joy in the game now had to balance that approach with another reality. With the university's fall term over and deployment six days away, the majority of V-12 trainees had been granted furloughs to return home and see loved ones before shipping off. Allowing the members of his team to do the same would severely hinder their ability to prepare for Wisconsin.

For Burnham, there was really no choice at all. He told the men on his squad to head for home if they so desired and meet back up in Chicago Friday evening. They would gather once again at the Edgewater Beach hotel on the north side of Chicago's lakefront, where they would have a blackboard scouting session as a team to prepare for Wisconsin. A large portion of the team took him up on the offer and headed for the hills, leaving Burnham and his staff with a skeleton crew to get ready for the Badgers.[5]

Many of the men went home for a few days including Agase and Butkovich. Agase returned to Evanston which happened to be just a few miles from the Edgewater Beach Hotel, allowing him a little bit of extra time with his family before rejoining the squad.[6] Butkovich, meanwhile, headed for his tiny central Illinois hometown of St. David. But the star fullback made a pit-stop along the way to see his little brother and his former team.[7]

On that Wednesday afternoon in late October, Butkovich snuck through the canvas-wrapped fence surrounding Illinois' practice field to surprise the Fighting Illini and his former coach Ray Eliot with a quick visit. Eliot was in the middle of explaining a complicated play to his squad when Butkovich approached in his Marine uniform.

"I don't believe you," shouted Butkovich, grinning from ear to ear while interrupting the coach's tutoring session.

"Get out of here," replied Eliot, not skipping a beat. "What'd they do, transfer you back to Illinois?" Eliot began laughing and reached out to shake the hand of his former pupil. Importantly, Eliot reached for Butkovich's left hand as his right hand was injured from the Iowa game. He explained that the injury to his hand made it tough to catch a pass or a lateral anywhere but "in the guts".[8] The injury also likely had something to do with his issues fumbling the ball against the Hawkeyes.

Butkovich stood and watched practice sharing stories and enjoying what little time he had with his former coaches and teammates. He included a tale from the Iowa game about Agase, a fellow former Illini star and his best friend.

"Aggie was breaking up every line play and had the jump on those Iowa backs every time," Butkovich said. "And what happens but Aggie gets a letter from Appleby (Iowa's center) and some of the other Iowa players the other day asking how he could tell where every play was going. It was simple for Aggie...the Iowa linemen would alternate on every play. First, they'd block to the right, then to the left. It was a cinch to see that."[9]

A nearby reporter decided to try and get Butkovich to spill secrets of Purdue's success, inquiring about practice habits of the Boilermakers. Tony replied that his new team rarely scrimmaged each other and that each practice session usually included extended periods where players would switch positions and play touch football. "I play guard and Aggie plays in the backfield...we always have lots of fun," Tony added. "It's a good idea too. No danger of injuries before a game. We do all our scrimmaging on Saturday's."[10]

One former teammate of Tony's with the 1942 Illini squad was there to congratulate him on his successful campaign. With typical humility, Butkovich replied, "Behind that Purdue line anybody could run like I have."[11]

And while many observers had called the Purdue front wall the best in the nation, Touchdown Tony still had an uncanny nose for the end zone. Through six games, he had scored 13 touchdowns on the season including ten in Purdue's three conference games. He was also among the nation's leaders in rushing with 686 yards through six games and rushing average, gaining just a hair over six yards be carry. Burnham's T-formation suited Butkovich perfectly and Touchdown Tony was drawing comparisons to some of the all-time greats in the Big Ten. One columnist said Butkovich reminded him a lot of Pat Harder, the future NFL MVP who had starred at Wisconsin.[12] Several others said Tony reminded them of the great Tommy Harmon who had won the Heisman Trophy while at Michigan.[13]

Whatever historical comparisons were being made, Butkovich and his teammates had their eye on history itself. With ten touchdowns through three conference games, Tony had scored 60 points on the year. The league record was 72 points, set by Iowa All-American Gordon Locke in 1922, the year Butkovich was born, and nearly equaled by the legendary Red Grange at Illinois two years later.[14] The Galloping Ghost finished his myth-making 1924 season with 11 conference scores. Butkovich could tie the record with a pair of touchdowns against Wisconsin and surpass the record with any sort of score beyond that. It would be one more motivating factor for the game in Madison, for a team filled with them.

Back on campus, Coach Burnham was making the best of a very bad week. A skeleton crew of about 25 players had stuck around, mostly men who would not be deploying following the game with the Badgers. Burnham was losing some very important pieces to his team, no doubt. Agase, Butkovich and Genis would be impossible to replace but there was still a lot of talent on the team. Vacanti and Dimancheff would continue to run the offensive backfield and Kasap, Barwegen and Poremba were the foundation of a very good front line. And with the first wave of V-12 men leaving, there was a second wave coming in behind them including a pair of promising young men for Burnham to mentor.[15]

Freshmen V-12 trainees James Lockwood and Chalmers "Bump" Elliott had become available for Coach Burnham after spending their requisite first 16-weeks as students only. Lockwood was a center from Hinsdale, Ill., while Elliott came to Purdue from Bloomington, Ill., and was hoping to make his mark in the Boilermaker backfield. Both men were hoping to make an immediate impact and were added to the travel roster straight away. Three other newcomers joined the team after receiving medical discharge from the service and re-enrolling at the university. Halfbacks Jerry Mullin and Donald Schrenk and fullback Joe Winkler would also be making their first road trip after joining the team earlier that same week.[16]

When Friday rolled around, the three-dozen men of the travel squad met with the coaches and support staff at the Edgewater Beach Hotel north of downtown Chicago. It was the third time the team had convened at the landmark hotel, having stayed there earlier in the fall prior to games at Great Lakes Naval Station and Marquette. The Edgewater was one of Chicago's real jewels in the 1940s as it regularly hosted guests from Lena Horne and Charlie Chaplin to President Franklin D. Roosevelt. The ballroom often featured the likes of Benny Goodman, Tommy Dorsey and Glenn Miller and their orchestras. The hotel even had a 1,200-foot private beach along Lake Michigan and featured seaplane service to and from downtown Chicago for folks who didn't want to battle the traffic along Lake Shore Drive and those who preferred to arrive in style.[17]

Of course, the Boilermakers weren't at the Edgewater to enjoy any of those amenities. Instead, they were looking for a nice meal and a good night's rest before continuing on to the Wisconsin state capital the next morning. The coaching staff led the team through a classroom scouting session to get them ready for Wisconsin, a team which no one figured would give the Boilermakers much resistance. The Badgers were 1-5 on the year and hadn't scored a point in their last two games, losses to Notre Dame and Indiana. This opponent was a far cry from the 1942 Badger squad that had finished third in the country with an 8-1 record, including a win over national champion Ohio State. The roster, like so many others, had been decimated by the draft and the school had not been chosen as a Marine training station.

Still the Badgers were led by coach Harry Stuhldreher, one of the famed "Four Horsemen" of Notre Dame in the early 1920s under

Knute Rockne. Stuhldreher would have his team ready to play, whether they were undermanned or not. The Wisconsin skipper got an assist from the Chicago and Northwestern Railroad. Delays on the lines led the Boilermakers to not arrive in Madison until 40 minutes before kickoff. Cabs lined up along the curb at the depot and the Boilermakers frantically packed into the cars for the ten-minute ride to Camp Randall Stadium, all dressed in full uniform.[18]

In previous years, it was typical for most football teams, the Boilermakers amongst them, to board trains on Thursday nights for overnight rides to their destination. At the very least, they would plan to arrive in the opposing city by early Friday afternoon for a practice in the stadium and a more leisurely Friday evening followed by a travel-stress free Saturday morning. However, wartime travel restrictions affected most programs in some way. For teams that included military personnel, there were very specific rules in place regarding travel. When the Department of the Navy agreed to let V-12 participants partake in intercollegiate athletics, one of the stipulations was that trainees only be allowed 48-hour leave including travel.

This meant no Thursday-night departures for teams and, in some cases, whirlwind trips. For the Boilermakers, on this day, it put them under the gun despite the fact that Madison is relatively close to West Lafayette. The last few Purdue players didn't arrive to the stadium until about 25 minutes before kickoff. Tom Hughes, the reserve tackle who handled place kicking duties, lined up to get the game started after what had been a wild 24 hours of travel. He was one of the Boilermakers departing the following week so he had headed home to St. Louis for a few days with his family. In addition to the hectic train trip, Hughes had awakened the previous day in St. Louis and flown to Chicago to join the team. He was as happy as anyone to get the game started, the madness of the road behind him.[19]

Neither team did much in the early going, the Boilermakers letting a roughing the kicker penalty extend an early Wisconsin possession. But when Lew Rose jumped on a fumble by Wisconsin's Ray Dooney, the sudden change put the Boilermakers in business. The first snap after the turnover, Butkovich took a toss around the right end and outran everyone to the end zone, 33-yards and one step towards the record book.

Holding penalties hampered the Boilermakers for much of the first half and the Badgers continued to put up a fight. Midway through the second quarter, after forcing another punt, the Purdue offense put together a vintage drive. Thirteen plays and 67 yards later, Butkovich crashed into the end zone from four yards out and had tied the Big Ten season scoring record. With the first half waning, Wisconsin decided to try to get on the board with their passing game. It was ill-advised as Purdue tackle John Genis threw his hands high and intercepted the ball. Genis, another Marine playing in his final game of the season, lumbered toward the end zone, living out every lineman's dream. Sadly for Genis, he also lived out nearly every lineman's reality as he was tackled from behind at the 6-yard line. The sudden change had thrown the Purdue offense off as they got just one snap off in the final 51-seconds after the turnover and they had to settle for a 13-0 lead at the break.

As the home crowd slowly started to turn its allegiance away from their team and towards history, the most impressive thing about the Boilermakers' second half was how completely unified their effort was in trying to attain the record for their star fullback. Genis had the unconventional defensive lineman interception late in the first half. Babe Dimancheff got an interception of his own late in the third quarter, wiping out Wisconsin's best scoring chance of the day. Moments later he scampered 46 yards to pay dirt, giving Butkovich the first of two chances to kick his way to the scoring record.

The Purdue defense forced eight Wisconsin turnovers, intercepting five passes and hopping on three fumbles. That included second-half fumble recoveries by Dick Barwegen and Alex Agase. The all-for-one mentality included a perfectly executed onside kick by Hughes and a recovery by Dimancheff late in the fourth quarter, to say nothing of the courage Coach Burnham showed in bucking convention by going for the onside try to begin with. And in the ultimate measure of selflessness, defensive back Sam Vacanti deliberately gave up the opportunity for a score to give his teammate one more chance.

With less than two minutes to play and Wisconsin facing a third-and-long situation, Vacanti stepped in front of a Badger pass and grabbed an interception. Vacanti broke a tackle and seemed destined for the day's final score but as he reached the ten-yard line, he slowed up, allowing a Wisconsin player to catch him and bring him down at the five.

When Tony crossed the goal line for the final time two plays later, breaking a 21-year-old scoring record with 72 points in just four games, it may have been his name that entered the record books. But it was a record that belonged to the entire squad.

The win improved the Purdue record to 7-0 with two games remaining. As the team boarded the train to return to Chicago and West Lafayette beyond that, Butkovich struggled to take his jersey off. In a replay of the scene from the previous season after helping the Fighting Illini upset mighty Minnesota, the young man from central Illinois simply didn't want the afternoon to end.

Hughes and Genis led the team in several rounds of sing-a-longs on the train ride, including harmonizing multiple renditions of "Hail Purdue!", their adopted university's fight song.[20] Hughes, a Missouri man, and Genis, the intended captain for the Fighting Illini, came together perfectly to celebrate the school they had grown so fond of in just four months.

As the train pulled into the Big Four station in downtown Lafayette, the fare-thee-wells were difficult. It had been such a short time together, but a powerful one. As players and coaches said goodbye to the nine departing Marines, plenty of tears were shed.[21] It was fitting that, when it came time to organize the university's outgoing contingent of 57 Marines that evening, backup quarterbacks Jimmy Darr and Blaine Hibler were chosen as platoon leaders.[22]

While the team that would remain headed across the river and up the hill to campus, the nine Boilermakers who had played their final game for Purdue caught a midnight train out of town, destination Parris Island, S.C.[23]

CHAPTER 14

| WEEK EIGHT |
AT MINNESOTA

As he turned his attention to the next series of challenges at hand, namely figuring out his roster on the fly while preparing for a road game at Minnesota, Coach Elmer Burnham would do so with the highest ranked team in program history. The resounding win over Wisconsin certainly helped, but the Boilermakers had risen to the second spot in the Associated Press poll due in part to other results around the country the previous week.[1]

Top-ranked Notre Dame had faced off with No. 3 Navy in an epic showdown in Cleveland. The Fighting Irish got three touchdown passes from Angelo Bertelli in his final game before shipping off to Island in a 33-7 route of the Midshipmen in front of 82,000 fans at Cleveland Stadium. Meanwhile, second-ranked Army played to a 13-13 tie against sixth-ranked Penn. In front of a crowd registering at more than 71,000 people at Franklin Field in Philadelphia, the Cadets couldn't get future Heisman Trophy winner Glenn Davis loose and had to settle for the tie.

With the two teams immediately ahead of them in the polls finding their first blemishes of the season, the Boilermakers climbed to the

No. 2 spot, though Notre Dame had a stranglehold on the top ranking, receiving 97 of 101 first-place votes. Another stiff challenge awaited the Irish in the coming week as they would head to New York City to take on Army in Yankee Stadium. It would be a chance for the Irish to strengthen their grip even further on the top spot. And if they faltered, it would give the Boilermakers a chance at the top spot for the first time ever, assuming Purdue could take care of business in Minneapolis.

Of course, for Burnham, there were no givens at this point in the season. On top of having to figure out what his new roster looked like, Burnham had to wait a couple of extra days to work with the squad. Furloughs were still in place even when the team returned from Wisconsin on Sunday and several members of the team took advantage by getting away from campus for a few days. They didn't reconvene until Wednesday, Nov. 3, just four days prior to kickoff at Minnesota.[2]

That left Burnham and his staff with little more to do for two days than break down scouting reports of the Golden Gophers and try to put together a game plan.[3] The Gophers had been hit as hard as anyone by the redistribution of football talent due to the war. The university had been selected as a V-12 institution but only for engineering and premedical trainees. That meant All-American fullback Bill Daley, who was a Marine trainee, had to be transferred. Daley wound up at the University of Michigan for the 1943 season.[4] Daley was probably the most important Gopher to be transferred but he wasn't the only one. When the team opened fall training camp, it did so with a roster of just 23 players, only a handful of which had previous experience. It was a far cry from the 1942 team that had spent most of the season ranked.

And perhaps worse than losing their star player, the Gophers lost their head coach because of the war as well. Bernie Bierman coached Minnesota for a decade, leading the program to five national championships in that time, including back-to-back titles in 1940 and 1941.[5] Following the attack on Pearl Harbor, Bierman returned to the Marines with whom he had served in WWI. Coach Bierman became Lt. Col. Bierman and was put in charge of the athletics department and named the head football coach at Iowa Pre-Flight. But in early 1943, the Navy reversed course and he got his orders to head to sea.[6]

In all, the 1943 Gophers had to overcome a lot just to field a team.

Still, they opened the season strong by winning their first three over Missouri, Nebraska and Camp Grant. But successive blow-out losses to Michigan and Northwestern left the Gophers at 3-2 as they prepared for a homecoming showdown with Purdue.

One positive for the Boilermakers was the expected return of halfback Stan Dubicki, out for nearly a month since suffering a knee injury against Camp Grant. In addition to adding some experience to the backfield, Dubicki figured to resume his kicking duties since his replacement, Tom Hughes, had been transferred with the rest of the Marines. Another bright spot for Purdue was the emergence of Babe Dimancheff, who was finally starting to get national attention.[7] The civilian transfer from Butler had gained 436 yards on 71 carries with four touchdowns in his supporting role of Butkovich. Now he would have a chance to become the star of Burnham's backfield.

The coaching staff spent the bulk of Wednesday practice trying different combination in the backfield to find one that clicked in the T-formation offense that relied on multiple fakes and very precise timing to be effective. George Mihal and Bump Elliott took turns at fullback while Jack Butt and Don Lehmkuhl had the unenviable task of trying to replace Agase at the right guard position. Wells Ellis and Bob Plavo had the inside track on taking over for Genis at right tackle.[8]

The outstanding end combination of Joe Buscemi and Frank Bauman were also expected to miss the game at Minnesota with injuries.[9] And the top replacement at the spot, Bill O'Keefe, had left with the Marines. Suddenly, the seven-man front wall that just weeks ago had been called maybe the greatest collection of talent in Big Ten history was completely decimated. Just two of the seven were expected to play against the Gophers, Dick Barwegen and Mike Kasap.

After Wednesday practice, Burnham announced the appointment of Barwegen as the team captain for the remainder of the season.[10] The veteran was the only remaining holdover from the 1942 Purdue team and seemed a fitting choice to fill the vacancy of Agase and Genis, the two men who had served as captains for the first seven games. It helped that Barwegen was having an outstanding season and was gaining acclaim as one of the nation's best interior linemen. But more importantly, he had the respect of his teammates. Said one after the announcement,

"The most underrated man on this team is Dick Barwegen. He's the best lineman I've seen since I started playing college football."[11]

Following a brief practice Friday morning, the team headed to the station to once again hop on a northbound train. The Boilermakers arrived in the Twin Cities late Friday night to temperatures in the 30s and snow, conditions not uncommon in Minneapolis in early November, but it could make for sloppy playing conditions.[12] The field at Memorial Stadium was pretty well saturated by the week's precipitation and the surface hadn't been covered all week.[13] To make matters worse, the snow was of the heavy, slushy variety and it wouldn't take long for the field to turn into a muddy mess.

The Boilermakers tried to set the tone early with their best drive of the day. After teams traded punts to begin the game, the Boilermakers drove 60 yards for an early score. It was attack by committee as Vacanti, Elliott and Dimancheff each registered rushes of 11 yards or more on the drive. On fourth and goal from the one, the fresh-faced Elliott followed Barwegen through the left guard spot and into the end zone. Dubicki added the point after and the Boilermakers were out to 7-0 lead. As dominant as the squad had been on the drive, no one would've predicted the struggle ahead.

Minnesota drove deep into Purdue territory early in the second quarter but were turned away. Moments later, Elliott fumbled a snap on a fourth-down punt attempt and the Gophers got the ball back at midfield. The Gophers once again drove deep into Purdue territory only to see Elliott intercept a pass in the end zone. But once again, the great defensive effort didn't translate to offensive momentum for Purdue as the ensuing drive stalled again.

The Gophers again got the ball near midfield and slowly pushed forward. From the Boilermaker 44-yard line, fullback Hoyt Moncrief took a handoff up the middle and was met by a hard-charging Dimancheff. When Dimancheff collided with the Gopher runner, the ball went flying. Seconds later, Minnesota halfback Chuck Avery scooped up the loose ball, lifted his head and saw nothing but open field in front of him. He covered the final 36 yards untouched and as the game reached halftime, the score was knotted up at 7-7.

Snow continued to fall in the third quarter and field conditions continued to deteriorate. Neither team was able to move the ball or make much of an attempt to threaten to break the tie. Early in the fourth quarter, the Gophers seemed to catch a game-defining break. Frank Bauman, playing for the first time since the Ohio State game and still noticeably limping on a sore ankle, dropped back to punt after another stalled drive. But the wet ball never quite got to him and by the time Bauman was able to coral the ball and get the punt off, it was blocked by two Minnesota defenders. The ball careened out of bounds at the Purdue 14-yard line.

On first down, Moncrief gained five yards down to the nine but he was stopped cold on second down. On third-and-five from the nine, Cates picked up two yards and the Gophers had a decision to make. Facing a fourth-and-three from inside the opponent's ten, the Gophers could've tried a field goal to take the lead. But with unfavorable field conditions and their regular kicker on the sideline, the Gophers tried instead for the end zone. Once again, it was Bump Elliott making a huge play for the Purdue defense. Elliott was in coverage near the goal line and stepped in front of Minnesota end Verne Gagne for his second interception of the afternoon, once again thwarting the Gophers with a turnover in the end zone.

Purdue gained a pair of first downs but once again stalled out around midfield and Bauman came in to punt the ball away with less than three minutes to go. It appeared to the men on the field and the more than 40,000 fans in the stands that the game was destined to end in a tie. The Gophers took over at their 20 and took their time running their next three plays. However, they gained just eight yards and were forced to punt, this time with less than a minute to go. And suddenly, the problem of a wet ball, a slippery field and a difficult punt snap that nearly proved disastrous for the Boilermakers earlier was Minnesota's problem.

The snap from center bounced on the way back to freshman quarterback/punter Bill Peterson, then bounced away from the Gopher. Boilermaker captain Barwegen pounced on the ball and the Boilermaker offense had the ball on the 19-yard line with 48 seconds remaining. with one more chance to save the game and the dream of an undefeated season.

Purdue quarterback Sam Vacanti settled under center and on the first play, dropped back and swung a pass to the flat, aiming for end Charlie Haag, but came up short. Incomplete. Three more chances now for the Boilermakers. On second down, with halfback Dimancheff split wide to the right as a flanker, Vacanti once again dropped back to throw. This time he relied on Babe's speed to beat a Minnesota defender and catch up to the ball. Dimancheff got a step on Avery and as he pulled past the Gopher defender, Babe reached out to catch a perfectly delivered pass from Vacanti in stride about five yards deep in the end zone. Dimancheff reached up with one hand and drew the ball into his stomach as he tumbled out the back of the end zone. As he picked himself up from the muddy, semi-frozen turf, Babe was stone-faced, even as his teammates mobbed him in jubilation.

With half a minute to play, the Boilermakers had taken a 14-7 lead in one of the most improbable ways imaginable for a game being played in a blizzard: a perfectly executed 19-yard touchdown pass. The Gophers received the kick and ran one play to nowhere as time expired. The Boilermakers had survived, perfect record intact.

"How the heck did that happen," wondered Gagne after the game in a refrain that became common amongst his teammates.[14] The freshman end was in the middle of a breakout season with the Gophers. He would go on to earn All-Big Ten honors on the gridiron and get drafted by the Chicago Bears. Gagne also starred on the wrestling mat for the Gophers, winning two NCAA titles while at Minnesota. He would eventually pass up the opportunity to play for the Bears in favor of becoming one of the most important figures in the history of professional wrestling. As the eventual owner of the American Wrestling Association in Minneapolis, Gagne helped launch the careers of Hulk Hogan, Ric Flair, Shawn Michaels and dozens of others.[15] But on this afternoon, he was just another Golden Gopher in awe of what he'd just witnessed up close.

The Gophers had actually outgained the Boilermakers on the day and had used an effective punting game to win the field position battle for most of the afternoon. Until that final, fateful mishap and the picture-perfect Purdue pass that closed out the contest. The Boilermakers headed for the dressing room to get out of their mud-caked uniforms and prepare for the long ride home. And as it turned out, they just beat Mother Nature out of town.

The steady snow throughout the game continued after and by Sunday evening had turned into a full-blown blizzard. More than a foot of snow blanketed the Twin Cities to go along with 40 mph wind gusts. It took the city two days to clear the streets and made travel extremely difficult.[16] The Purdue squad had escaped Minnesota in more ways than one.

The Boilermakers weren't the only Top Ten team being pushed to the brink. While Notre Dame had dominated third-ranked Army in Yankee Stadium, shutting out the Cadets 26-0, fourth-ranked USC and No. 5 Penn both lost. The Trojans were upset by San Diego while the Quakers lost to seventh-ranked Navy. Sixth-ranked Michigan handled Indiana and Iowa Pre-Flight stayed undefeated by taking down Marquette.

When the latest Associate Press poll was released, the top two remained with Notre Dame claiming all 101 of the first-place votes. Purdue was solidly in second while Navy, Michigan and Iowa Pre-Flight rounded out the Top Five.[17]

The Boilermakers had just one more opponent standing between them and perfection. But like everything else the team had faced in recent weeks, the battle for the Old Oaken Bucket would present a unique set of challenges. And it would be anything but easy.

CHAPTER 15

| WEEK NINE |
AT INDIANA

Fresh off the thrilling win at Minnesota, coach Elmer Burnham and his staff found themselves in an unusual situation. They had some down time, thanks to an open week in their schedule. The Boilermakers had been slated to play Michigan State in a non-conference game on November 13, but when the Spartans canceled their season, it left a hole in the Purdue schedule. Burnham and his athletic director, Red Mackey, had tried to fill the spot so the Boilermakers could play a full schedule. They had been in talks with Marquette to have a return date at Ross-Ade Stadium to complete a unique home and home series as both teams had an open date on Nov. 13. But the Hilltoppers' season had gone sideways since the first meeting in Milwaukee and discussions went nowhere. Marquette ended up losing three of their final four games to close out the season at 3-4-1.

As fate would have it, despite their best efforts, the Boilermakers' inactivity actually cost them in the eyes of Associated Press voters.

Top-ranked Notre Dame continued to lead the way after defeating Northwestern 25-6. And every other team in the top five won as well, with No. 3 Navy dominating Columbia 61-0, No. 4 Michigan shutting out Wisconsin 27-0 and No. 5 Iowa Pre-Flight handling Camp Grant 28-13. When the new poll was announced, Iowa Pre-Flight had vaulted from fifth to second, knocking the idle Boilermakers down to the third spot in the nation. Michigan remained fourth and Navy fell to fifth.[1] While the Seahawks' meteoric rise may not have made much sense at first glance, they had a perfect 8-0 record on the season. For the more cynical observer, the speculation was that Iowa Pre-Flight had risen so quickly in order to set up a No. 1 vs. No. 2 showdown as they were slated to play Notre Dame next.

With no one to play, Burnham gave his squad the Monday after the Minnesota game off. The coaches, meanwhile, didn't have that luxury. Assistant coach Cecil Isbell was still trying to figure out the best combinations for his backfield. Fellow assistant Joe Dienhart continued to evaluate the play of his new linemen, looking for the right men to fill the spots of Genis and Agase for one final game.[2]

Burnham was pleased with his team's effort at Minnesota and the resolve they'd shown under extreme circumstances in the past week. But he knew well the challenge ahead.

"We have a long way to go to get ready for an Indiana squad that has been working together as a unit all fall," Burnham said while meeting with reporters Monday afternoon.[3] He had a roster full of men who hadn't stepped foot on a varsity field until the past few months, some of whom hadn't even put on a jersey until the previous week. And by all accounts, Indiana had one of the strongest civilian teams in the country.

So strange was the 1943 season that the script of the entire season had flipped. While teams like Purdue, Michigan, Notre Dame and Northwestern had gotten an early boost from their participation in the Navy's V-12 program, they all took massive hits in the middle of the season. Meanwhile, Indiana didn't have the benefit of the military personnel but also did not have to deal with the upheaval of losing key contributors.

Veteran Indiana coach Bo McMillin had a solid team and they got off to a great start to the 1943 season. After starting the season with a tie against Miami University and a tough loss at Northwestern, the Hoosiers found their footing. Or, rather, they found their aerial attack.

Consecutive wins over Wabash and Nebraska saw Indiana put 52 and 54 points on the board, respectively. A 7-7 tie against Iowa was followed by two more dominant wins over Wisconsin and Ohio State. The Hoosiers entered the final month of the season with a 4-1-2 record. Unfortunately for them, it was the most difficult stretch of their season as they dropped a game at Michigan and a game at home against Great Lakes.

Burnham knew the biggest challenge against the Hoosiers would be to slow down their explosive offense and that meant trying to find a way to defend freshman quarterback Bob "Hunchy" Hoernschemeyer. The rookie out of Cincinnati had taken advantage of the NCAA's ruling to allow freshmen to play right away and promptly came in and set the college world on fire. Hoernschemeyer led the nation in passing yards and total yards and his connection with end Pete Pihos had helped make the latter into an All-America selection in 1943.[4] Hoernschemeyer was having such a fine season that Indiana athletics director W.H. Tom proclaimed him the best player he'd seen in 17 years on the job in Bloomington.[5]

The teams would be renewing their annual rivalry for the "Old Oaken Bucket", a traveling trophy that had been introduced to the series in 1925 by a joint agreement of both schools' alumni associations in Chicago.[6] The adoption of the trophy itself was inspired by a poem by Samuel Woodworth of the same name:

> How dear to this heart are the scenes of my childhood,
> When fond recollection presents them to view!
> The orchard, the meadow, the deep-tangled wild-wood,
> And every loved spot which my infancy knew!
> The wide-spreading pond, and the mill that stood by it,
> The bridge, and the rock where the cataract fell,
> The cot of my father, the dairy-house nigh it,
> And e'en the rude bucket that hung in the well-
> The old oaken bucket, the iron-bound bucket,
> The moss-covered bucket which hung in the well
>
> That moss-covered vessel I hail as a treasure;
> For often, at noon, when returned from the field,

I found it the source of an exquisite pleasure,
The purest and sweetest that nature can yield.
How ardent I seized it, with hands that were glowing!
How quick to the white-pebbled bottom it fell;
Then soon, with the emblem of truth over-flowing,
And dripping with coolness, it rose from the well –
The old oaken bucket, the iron-bound bucket,
The moss-covered bucket arose from the well.

How sweet from the green mossy brim to receive it,
As, poised on the curb, it inclined to my lips!
Not a full blushing goblet could tempt me to leave it,
Though filled with the nectar that Jupiter sips.
And now, far removed from the loved situation,
The tear of regret will intrusively swell,
As fancy reverts to my father's plantation,
And sighs for the bucket which hangs in the well –
The old oaken bucket, the iron-clad bucket,
The moss-covered bucket which hangs in the well." [7]

All in attendance felt that the sentiment of the poem perfectly captured a simpler time and the nostalgic feelings they had for the mostly rural and overwhelmingly agrarian Indiana, even though Woodworth himself was from Massachusetts and the poem was about his childhood New England home.

The final game of the 1943 season would be the 46th meeting between the two in-state rivals, with Purdue holding the overall edge 24-16-5. The Boilermakers also had a slight edge in trophy games, having hung 10 iron P's from the handle to Indiana's six. The teams had tied twice, including in the first Bucket game, a 0-0 tie in 1925 in Bloomington.

Neither Burnham nor McMillin had played in the rivalry but both had experienced it on the sidelines since the mid-30s and were well acquainted with its intensity. The schools had split the previous dozen meetings, with most of those results being decided by less than a touchdown. The Hoosiers got the better of things in 1942 with a 20-0 win, their largest margin of victory in nearly three decades. Indiana was certainly hoping for more of the same to close out the 1943 campaign.

Both teams set about getting ready for the rivalry in their own ways. With the weather outside taking a turn for the worse, Burnham moved practices indoors, utilizing the fieldhouse once more.[8] He continued to sort through his personnel and the squad focused mainly on improving the timing of offensive plays. With a smaller team now, the Boilermakers would hope to rely on speed more than power. Stan Dubicki and Dick Bushnell were undersized at the left halfback spot, each weighing just over 150 pounds. The Purdue offense also spent a bit more time working on the passing game, hoping to take advantage of the fact that Frank Bauman would be rejoined by Joe Buscemi, back from injury, to form a powerful receiving duo.

Following Wednesday's practice, Burnham let the reporters in attendance know the reconstruction project was still underway.

"We're still trying to determine our most effective combination," he said. "And we probably won't make a definite decision on the starting lineup until just before game time."[9]

No matter the personnel, the Boilermakers had spent a significant portion of the previous two weeks getting ready for Indiana's aerial attack. Defensively, they had held up well against the pass all season long, allowing just 29 completed passes on 98 combined attempts to opponents. What's more, opposing offenses only averaged about 50 passing yards per game versus the Boilermakers. Hoernschemeyer, meanwhile, had thrown for more than a thousand yards on the season, averaging 127 passing yards per game. He would easily be the best quarterback the Purdue squad had seen all year.

Indiana, meanwhile, held closed-door practices all week, not allowing any outsiders to see what they were cooking up to get the edge.[10] McMillin did extensive work with the defense, trying to prepare them for the intricacies of Purdue's T-formation and all of the options Vacanti would have at his disposal. And they continued to work on the passing game with Hoernschemeyer pulling the trigger. As gameday approached, the Hoosiers began to feel more confident. Their roster was as healthy as it had been in a month. They were prepared and eager to spoil the Boilermaker bid at perfection and ensure Purdue would not earn a share of the conference crown.

Burnham settled on his 36-man travel squad and after a light practice on Friday morning the team headed out for McCormick's Creek State Park, located near Spencer, Indiana. The beautifully appointed Canyon Inn on the grounds of the state park would serve as the overnight accommodations for the squad, just 14 miles to the west of Indiana's Bloomington campus.[11]

It was customary for teams to travel the day before games, even for such a short trip to take on an in-state rival. It would be one last time for this group of Boilermakers to hit the road together with no distractions from the goal at hand. And the journey itself was uneventful, even pleasant. The same could not always be said for this trip.

* * * * *

Forty years earlier, the Boilermakers and the Hoosiers had decided to play the yearly rivalry on a neutral site in Indianapolis. It was the first game in the burgeoning rivalry to be contested away from campus, slated to be held at Washington Park on the east side of the city. On the morning of the game, two Purdue Specials had been commissioned from the Big Four Railroad to bring the team and more than 1,500 fans down the line to Indianapolis.[12]

As the first train approached downtown, tragedy struck. The lead car, carrying some 950 passengers including the team and more than 600 students, rounded a curve at the Mill Street Power House and collided with a coal car on the same track. Because of a miscommunication amongst train officials, the coal car did not know about the specials coming down the line and didn't know to leave the path open. The Purdue Special was traveling at around 25 miles per hour when the collision happened. The engine was driven underneath the coal cars and the first passenger car, made mostly of wood, split from end to end and exploded into the air, a rain of splinters and twisted metal falling back to earth.[13]

When the dust had settled, 16 lay dead in the rubble with several dozen more injured. Another man died hours later from injuries sustained in the wreck bringing the death toll to 17. Fourteen were members of the Purdue football team, representing more than one-fourth of the entire team. Among the injured was Lafayette native Harry G. Leslie. The fullback, team captain and student body president was so gravely injured that he was actually pronounced dead and taken to the makeshift morgue just off site. While there, Leslie regained consciousness to everyone's amazement and slowly recovered from his injuries.[14] Nearly three decades later, Leslie was elected governor of the state of Indiana, the only Purdue alumnus to assume that office.

The Purdue train wreck is among the worst tragedies to ever befall a college athletics team and, for years after, it cast a pall over the Purdue-Indiana game. The rivalry game returned to Indianapolis a year later for what is still the only neutral-site meeting between the teams. And while the Boilermakers elected to travel via the Northwestern Traction line so they could avoid traversing the scene of the disaster, they were triumphant that afternoon, 27-0.[15]

* * * * *

Burnham and company were hoping for a similar triumph to close out their perfect season. The Boilermakers readied for the game in their sparkling white road jerseys with twin black stripes on each sleeve and gold leather helmets with three black winged stripes down the middle. Unseasonably warm weather put the temperature at kickoff in the low 60s but a stiff wind made it necessary for the Hoosiers to have a player hold the ball steady during the opening kickoff.[16] Babe Dimancheff received the kick and returned it to the 24-yard line. Burnham and Isbell decided to try some trickery on the first play with quarterback Sam Vacanti taking the snap and immediately pivoting to his right. He rifled a pass to Dimancheff who had set up wide to the right and ten yards behind the line, hoping to catch the defense off guard and take advantage of the halfback's speed. It didn't work as the Hoosiers were onto the play immediately, tackling Dimancheff for a five-yard loss. Purdue punted three plays later and a poor kick gave Indiana the ball near midfield.

Taking each snap from what would eventually become known as a shotgun formation, five yards deep in the backfield, Hoernschemeyer passed the Hoosiers down to the Purdue 21-yard line. On the sixth play of the drive, the Indiana signal caller dropped back to pass again but missed his mark badly, throwing right at Vacanti who grabbed maybe the easiest interception of his career at the 11-yard line. The Boilermakers still couldn't get anything going on offense and the teams traded punts, followed by a Purdue fumble. For the third time in the first quarter, the Hoosiers would start a drive at the midfield stripe.

Hoernschemeyer decided to take a shot and on the first play, dropped back to pass. He flung a beautiful ball nearly 50 yards in the air but overshot his man, Don Mangold, by about three yards. Once again, there was a Boilermaker defensive back there to take advantage as Bump Elliot snagged the interception at the five-yard line and returned it to the 26 before being pushed out of bounds. The second interception of the first quarter finally provided a spark for the Purdue attack.

With a healthy mix of Dimancheff and Elliot, the Purdue running game covered 41 yards in five plays, regularly changing the point of attack with inside rushes and sweeps around both ends. On second down from the Indiana 38, Purdue came out in a completely different formation. Vacanti lined up five yards deep next to Dimancheff with Elliot wide to the left. Right halfback Keith Parker actually lined up under center and then went in motion to the right before the snap. When Parker reached the end of the line, the ball was snapped back to Vacanti and right end Frank Bauman immediately released downfield on a pass pattern. This left his Indiana counterpart with a free rush, except Parker was now in position to pick up the block.

Bauman ran down field and cut across the middle of the field, wide open in the middle of three confused Indiana defensive backs. Bauman caught the pass at the 27-yard line and kept running towards the sideline where Elliott and left end Joe Buscemi were waiting to take out the final two Indiana defenders. Bauman settled in behind his wall of blockers and tight-roped the sideline all the way to the end zone. When Dubicki added the extra point, the Boilermakers ended the first quarter with a 7-0 lead.

The second stanza was marred on both sides by punts, turnovers and penalties, although both teams missed opportunities late in the frame. On third-and-long from their own 28, Dimancheff went in motion from his right halfback spot and at the snap, streaked downfield. Vacanti dropped back and hurled a deep ball to his halfback, who had gotten behind every member of the Indiana defense. But the ball was just out of reach as a leaping Dimancheff was barely able to get a fingertip on it as it fluttered to the ground. The Boilermakers had come close to taking a commanding lead but would be forced to punt.

Indiana got the ball back and promptly fumbled it away, giving the Boilermakers possession right back in the waning seconds of the half.

Perfect Warriors

After a tripping penalty set Purdue back 15 yards, they faced a first-and-25 form their own 38. Hoping to score once more before intermission, Vacanti dropped back to pass once more. He was again looking for Bauman on a crossing pattern 15-yards downfield but the ball was woefully underthrown. Indiana linebacker Pete Pihos, who would go on to a Hall of Fame career as an end with the Philadelphia Eagles, grabbed the interception and took off towards the goal line with two blockers and a whole lot of open field in front of him.

That's when the Indiana All-American made a fateful mistake. Instead of following his blockers, allowing them to clear the way as Bauman had done for the Boilermakers earlier in the game, Pihos got out ahead of his helpers. By the time he reached the 20-yard line, Pihos was all alone with four Boilermakers in pursuit. Vacanti, as he had done in a variety of ways all season, atoned for his mistake by taking a great angle to cut off Pihos at the 15-yard line. The Purdue quarterback dove at the Hoosier defender's legs and brought him down 10 yards short of the goal line as the halftime gun sounded.

Indiana had come close twice but still found themselves trailing 7-0 when they received the second half kickoff. The Hoosiers drove the ball to midfield before stalling out and being forced to punt. The Boilermakers once again narrowly avoided disaster. Dimancheff tried fielding the punt on the run and ended up dropping the ball. As he fell to the ground, Babe took a swipe at the ball, knocking it away from a pair of Hoosiers converging on the play, allowing Elliot to recover the ball.

The Purdue offense finally started to click with runs by Dimancheff, Elliott and Parker gaining 20 yards on four plays. Then Elliot took a hand-off through the left side of the line and cut back across the field, looking for an opening. He found the opening but lost the ball as Pihos once again came up with a great play, reaching out and stealing the pigskin from Elliot as Bump ran past. Another Purdue drive stalled because of a self-inflicted mistake.

Indiana's offense once again drove the ball deep before the Purdue defense stiffened. After a two-yard run and an incomplete pass, Indiana had third-and-goal from the 7-yard line. Hoernschemeyer rolled left, looking for an open man. Instead he found the combination of Bauman and Mike Kasap, who converged on the QB for a sack. On fourth-and-goal from the 14, Hoernschemeyer's desperation pass to the end zone was intercepted by Vacanti. Another Indiana turnover and another missed opportunity for the Hoosiers.

It became a field position battle for the rest of the third quarter with Purdue repeatedly failing to get the ball out of its own end. As the fourth quarter began, the Hoosiers had the ball, once again in positive territory and growing ever-more desperate for a game-tying score. A steady drive took a major move forward when fullback James Allerdice found a hole and scampered 15 yards to the 4-yard line. The Hoosiers seemed destined to finally draw even. But on the very next play, Indiana quarterback John Cannady ran right up the middle and as he fought for extra inches, lost the ball. Dimancheff pounced on it and Purdue took over.

Pinned deep and not wanting to give up a safety, which would cost Purdue two points and the ball, the Boilermakers elected to punt on first down and Elliot boomed one to the 50. But Indiana again took over in a great spot, a Hoernschemeyer punt return setting them up at the Purdue 33. After first down went nowhere, Hoernschemeyer dropped back on second down and popped a screen pass to John McDonnell that went all the way to the nine. Back to back run plays to the left got Indiana to the 3-yard line where they faced a third-and-goal situation. This time the call was for a sweep to the left and Allerdice was met at the line of scrimmage by a wall of Purdue defenders when Boilermaker reserve Joe Winkler ripped the ball from his hands and Purdue took over once more on the two.

This time, Burnham decided to drive out of trouble rather than kick away and his squad gained a two first downs before having to punt away. The Boilermakers had successfully flipped the field position and as Hoernschemeyer caught the punt at the Indiana 25, he was tackled immediately by Buscemi. With three minutes to go and now 72 yards away from tying the game, the situation looked dire for the home team. Hoernschemeyer dropped to pass on first down and it appeared Buscemi had him dead to rights for a sack but missed, Hunchy scrambling out of trouble for a nine-yard gain. After a first down, Hoernschemeyer dropped back to pass again and once again Buscemi closing in him, the Hoosier star was able to escape the sack once more. Hunchy let a pass fly down the sideline and Elliott leaped up to bat it down, swatting it with both hands. Instead of falling to the ground or flying out of bounds, the ball just popped up in the air, long enough for intended receiver Frank Hoppe to grab the ball and turn up field.

He was finally brought down at the 20 and the Hoosiers were still alive.

A screen pass for 12 yards moved the ball down to the Purdue 8 and gave Indiana a fresh set of downs. McDonnell took a sweep to the left on the next play and had a convoy to the end zone, three blockers leading the way. Kasap, Parker and Collings, played it perfectly, splitting the blockers and bringing McDonnell down a foot short of the goal line. A direct snap to the fullback on second down went nowhere as Allerdice was met a yard deep in the backfield by Barwegen for a short loss.

Seconds continued to tick off the clock as the grandstand began to spill onto the field, the home fans ringing the sidelines and end zone three deep, trying to will their men to victory. On third down, it was Allerdice to the right and he was once again stonewalled by the Purdue front seven. This time it was Dimancheff making initial contact and Vacanti finishing off the tackle, bringing up fourth and goal from the one-foot line.

With the Indiana run game unable to finish the deal, McMillin turned to his trusty passing attack to try and gain the final foot on fourth down. Hoernschemeyer took the snap, dropped back and paused for what felt to all in attendance like an eternity, hoping for someone to get open or the defense to make a fatal mistake. Neither happened and the final pass of the day fell to the ground just beyond the end line, far from the outstretched arms of the intended Hoosier receiver.

The Boilermaker defense had held. Three times in the second half, Indiana had been turned away after breeching the Purdue 10-yard line, including coming within feet of tying the game twice in the fourth quarter. As Vacanti settled under center with three seconds remaining, a quarterback sneak would end the game. But as the Purdue signal caller took the snap and was diving forward for the final play, the afternoon's frustration boiled over for Indiana. Linebacker John Cannady took a swing at Vacanti and connected flush on the Boilermaker's jaw, knocking him out cold there on the Memorial Stadium turf. It could be that Cannady was trying in desperation to knock the ball free and connected with Vacanti's face instead. No matter the reason, the outcome was a scary one. And it would, no doubt, add a touch more color to this already bitter rivalry in future years.

Vacanti came to and joined his team for the celebration. As the Boilermakers headed to the locker room, they were notified that this was the first shut-out suffered by Indiana since the 1939 season. There was much to be joyful about. They had won the Old Oaken Bucket back for Purdue. They had clinched a share of the Big Ten Conference title. And they had answered the call from Agase, Butkovich, Genis and all the rest, finishing what they had all started together five months earlier: a perfect season in West Lafayette.

CHAPTER 16

AFTER THE SEASON: THE COACHES

As the sun came up on Sunday morning after the victory over Indiana, the Boilermakers were content with the fact that they had done all they could. With the win over their in-state rival they had secured the Old Oaken Bucket for the first time in four seasons. They had locked up at least a share of the Big Ten title, the first in nearly a decade. And they had completed an undefeated, untied record for the first time since 1929. Now their attention would turn to the rest of the college football world as the regular season had one week to go for a select few teams.

While the Boilermakers were taking care of the Hoosiers in Bloomington, less than 200 miles due north in South Bend, the Fighting Irish were in an epic battle with Iowa Pre-Flight. The No. 1 vs. No. 2 showdown lived up to the hype with the Irish scoring late in the fourth quarter to pull out a 14-13 win, preserving their perfect record and leaving them atop the national polls. Fourth-ranked Michigan won handily against Ohio State to close out its season at 8-

1, the only blemish coming earlier in the year against Notre Dame, while No. 5 Navy had the week off to get ready for their annual showdown with Army.

When the new Associated Press poll was released, there was once again intrigue at the top. Notre Dame remained in the top spot but actually lost a few first-place votes. The Seahawks, despite the loss, impressed voters so much with their performance that they actually gained ground on the Irish and retained a first-place vote. With its rivalry win over Ohio State, Michigan moved up to third while the undefeated, untied Boilermakers slipped to fourth despite earning their own rivalry victory. Duke rounded out the top five, leapfrogging over a Navy team that had defeated the Blue Devils head-to-head earlier in the season.[1]

Duke, Michigan and Purdue had all completed their seasons as conference champions, Michigan and Purdue sharing the Big Ten crown. There were still a handful of games left to be contested including Notre Dame taking on Great Lakes Naval, Iowa Pre-Flight facing off with Minnesota and, of course, Army-Navy. The Midshipmen took care of the Cadets in West Point, defeating Army 13-0. Iowa Pre-Flight had little trouble with Minnesota, routing the Gophers 32-0. But the lack of drama in those two contests was more than made up for at Great Lakes Naval Station.

The Irish opened the game with a touchdown on their first possession but couldn't get anything else going and had to settle for a 7-0 lead at the half. The Bluejackets answered back with an opening-drive score in the second half to cut the lead to 7-6. Great Lakes scored again late in the third stanza to take a 12-7 lead and carried its advantage into the fourth quarter.[2]

But the Irish, backs against the wall, rose to the challenge. Notre Dame drove 80 yards on an astounding 20 plays, All-American halfback Creighton Miller crashing over the goal line with just over a minute remaining to give the road team a 14-12 lead. Notre Dame booted the ensuing kickoff out of bounds and the Bluejackets took over at their 35-yard line. A 19-yard pass on first down moved the ball into Notre Dame territory. Great Lakes snapped the ball with 38 seconds to go and halfback Steve Lach dropped back to pass, scrambled out of some pressure from the Irish pass rush, and heaved a ball downfield. All at once the 22,000 sailors at Ross Field saw the same thing; Great Lakes quarterback Paul Anderson all alone downfield, 15 yards clear of the nearest defender. Anderson caught the pass at the 5-yard line and trotted into the end zone. Great Lakes converted its first PAT of the day and with 28 seconds left in the season, led the Irish 19-14.[3]

In their last desperate effort, future Heisman Trophy winning quarterback Johnny Lujack, who had replaced 1943 Heisman winner Angelo Bertelli after he was called to Parris Island with Butkovich and Agase and all the rest, had his final pass of the season intercepted and the upset was complete. Great Lakes Naval Station, which had begun the season with a 23-13 loss to Purdue, had toppled the mighty Irish to close out the campaign.[4]

With the loss, Notre Dame fell to 9-1 on the season leaving Purdue as the only major football team with an undefeated, untied record in the nation. However, when the final AP Poll was released the following week, Notre Dame remained atop the rankings followed by Iowa Pre-Flight and Michigan. The Boilermakers finished in fifth, despite receiving the second-most first-place votes amongst pollsters. In the final three weeks of the season, Purdue had notched thrilling road wins at Minnesota and Indiana but had fallen from second in the country to fifth.[5] And all this even though two of the teams that would finish ahead of them lost in that same time frame.

The Boilermakers would have to settle for a share of the Big Ten title with an 8-1 Michigan squad as both had notched perfect records in conference play. At the time, the conference did not have a postgame bowl tie-in as the Big Ten and the Pacific Coast Conference were still three years away from partnering up for the annual Rose Bowl matchup.

In an interesting twist, the Rose Bowl itself would have a Purdue tie despite the Boilermakers not being invited. Due to wartime travel restrictions, the 1944 edition of the game would feature Southern California taking on conference rival Washington in a de facto conference title game. Given the geographic distance between the two, they hadn't played in the regular season so the match-up in the bowl game would determine the PCC champion as well. The Huskies were coached by Boilermaker legend Ralph "Pest" Welch, star fullback of the 1929 Purdue team that also went undefeated and won the Big Ten title. Welch had followed his former coach Jimmy Phelan to Seattle when Phelan left Purdue and then took over the program in 1942 after

Phelan was let go. Welch's Huskies hadn't played a game since the end of October and it showed as USC soundly defeated them 29-0.[6]

Back in West Lafayette, postseason awards began to roll in for the Boilermakers. Dick Barwegen, Alex Agase and Tony Butkovich were all named first-team all-conference while Frank Bauman and Mike Kasap were on the second team. Joe Buscemi, Bob Plevo, John Genis, Sam Vacanti and Babe Dimancheff all earned honorable mention all-conference.[7] Barwegen was voted the team MVP while Butkovich and Agase earned multiple All-America honors.[8,9]

With the season completed, attention within the program turned to preparations for the 1944 season. Spring practices began in mid-March and there were some familiar names in the group with Buscemi, Vacanti, Dimancheff, Elliott all returning. The Boilermakers were once again sharing training facilities with the Cleveland Indians but the uncertainty of being able to field a team for the coming season was gone. Some 90 players showed up for the first week of spring drills for the Boilermakers and the sessions culminated a month later with an intra-squad scrimmage in Ross-Ade Stadium.[10] But, as it turned out, the future would look drastically different for the team on the sidelines.

On May 14, 1944, head coach Elmer Burnham shocked the Purdue community when he resigned as the leader of the Boilermakers after just two seasons at the helm. Burnham accepted a head coaching job at the University of Rochester in upstate New York.[11] The move was a stunner.

"This has been a hard decision to make," Burnham said. "But after careful consideration it is with deep regret that I sever my connection with Purdue University. It has been a pleasure to serve under Red Mackey. However, I felt that the position offered to me by the University of Rochester presented an opportunity that could not be ignored."[12]

The opportunity Burnham referenced was a long-term contract at Rochester, a rarity at the time in the collegiate coaching ranks and nearly unheard of at the highest levels of the sport.[13] There were rumors, too, that Rochester had offered a handsome salary to Burnham, on par or surpassing what he was being paid at Purdue but official terms of the contract were not revealed.

Burnham was a great choice for Rochester on several different fronts. Sure, he had success at the highest level and he was the type of man to be enticed by longer-term stability over the glitz and glamour of competing at the highest levels of the game. But he also had his greatest success by harnessing a disparate group of Navy V-12 officers. Well, Rochester was a V-12 school as well, the football program made up largely of future sailors and Marines, and they found just the man to be able to succeed in those circumstances.

However, in making the hire, Rochester President Dr. Alan Valentine wanted to make clear that this was not a move toward trying to elevate the program into the upper echelon of the collegiate game. The school did not offer athletic scholarships, room and board or any other financial incentives to attract top athletes and it would not start, no matter where the head coach had been previously.[14]

That philosophy suited Burnham just fine. He had always been of the opinion that the purpose of sports, and football specifically, should be to have fun. There were lessons that could be gleaned along the way and physical activity was a good thing but one should play football for the enjoyment of the game. It was his approach with the YMCA and as a high school mentor at South Bend Central and it remained his attitude when he arrived at Purdue. It was one of the reasons his teams regularly took times to have fun and play games during practice throughout the 1943 season. The pressures of recruiting talented players and glad-handing notable donors didn't appeal to Burnham. He preferred to just coach and the move to Rochester would allow him to do just that. So, Burnham, his wife Grace and their three children moved to upstate New York.

As it turned out, it was the perfect match of university and educator as Elmer Burnham spent the next 17 seasons on the sidelines for the Yellowjackets and remains the program's all-time leader in wins. His 82-48-6 record included undefeated seasons in 1952 and 1958 and 17 of his players earned Little All-America honors at Rochester.[15]

Burnham's abrupt decision to leave Purdue put the Boilermakers in a tough spot. But there were no feelings of ill will. On the day the announcement was made, Mackey couldn't have been more gracious in accepting his football coach's resignation.

"I know that this was a hard decision for Elmer to make, and it was an even harder one for us to accept," Mackey said. "He certainly leaves with our best wishes for his continued success at Rochester."[16]

Mackey wasted little time in naming Burnham's successor. Just one day after Burnham headed to New York, Cecil Isbell was named the new head coach of the Boilermakers while Joe Dienhart was retained as the top assistant and line coach.[17] In a span of ten months, Isbell had gone from the starting quarterback for the Green Bay Packers to the head coach at his alma mater.

The former NFL passing champ led the Boilermakers for three seasons, from 1944-46, before making the leap to the next level. Given his youth and success as a player at all levels and now as a college coach, Isbell received offers to move to the professional ranks quite often while in West Lafayette. Following the 1946 season, he decided to take one. In February 1947, Isbell became the first head coach of the Baltimore Colts of the All-American Football Conference. After going 2-11-1 in his first season with the Colts, he led the team to a 7-7 record in 1948, tying the Buffalo Bills for the East division title. It was a solid season, with Isbell able to tutor another wily Texan in rookie quarterback and future Hall of Famer Y.A Tittle.[18]

Tittle was good but the best player for the Colts that season was a second-year guard out of Purdue University named Dick Barwegen. Barwegen was named an All-Pro that season, the first of four such honors in his great career.[19]

The 1949 season was expected to be a breakthrough for the Colts but after an 0-4 start, Isbell felt he had lost the team and resigned.[20] He landed in Chicago the next year as an assistant with the Cardinals, one of the founding members of the NFL. Isbell came to the Cardinals to reconnect with his old head coach, the Green Bay Packers' legendary founder Curly Lambeau.[21] After two seasons in Chicago, Isbell spent a year as an assistant with the Dallas Texans under Jimmy Phelan, then another year as an assistant at Louisiana State University.[22]

By the age of 40, Isbell was out of coaching. He moved back to Wisconsin, spending more than a decade as a sales representative with Safeway Steel. Various other business ventures took him across the country and he and his wife Alice finally settled near Chicago. He was inducted into the College Football Hall of Fame in 1967 and the Packers Hall of Fame in 1972. In 1985, after a long battle with kidney and liver disease, Isbell died at a Hammond, Ind., hospital. He was 69. Isbell was buried in West Lafayette, less than a mile from Ross-Ade Stadium.[23]

While Isbell made his way around the country in football and in business, his top assistant never left West Lafayette. Joe Dienhart had grown up in the Lafayette area, joining Burnham and the Boilermakers only after his program at St. Joseph's was shuttered. He remained an assistant football coach until 1953 and authored several books on coaching and scouting while also teaching in the physical education department at Purdue. When Dienhart moved out of coaching it was so he could spend more time on his administrative duties as an assistant athletic director in charge of ticketing, a position he held until he retired in 1971. Dienhart didn't stay idle for long, running for Mayor of West Lafayette and winning two terms. He remained in West Lafayette until his death in 1987 at age 83.[24]

Among Dienhart's duties while working in administration was to manage the Purdue Golf Courses, where he worked hand in hand with fellow 1943 assistant coach Sammy Voinoff. Voinoff stayed on staff with Isbell was well when Burnham left and remained an assistant with the football program until 1950. In 1951, Voinoff took over the head coaching duties of the golf team at Purdue and had as much success as any Boilermaker coach, in any sport, ever. For the next quarter century, Voinoff led one of the premier golf programs in the nation.

The Boilermakers won 10 Big Ten titles under his tutelage while three different players won NCAA Individual titles for Voinoff.[25] In 1961, with the NCAA Championships being hosted on Purdue's home course, the Boilermakers beat the field by 11 strokes.[26] The individual champion that year was Ohio State star Jack Nicklaus, but his Buckeyes were no match for the Purdue foursome. In addition to the 1961 team title, Voinoff's Boilermakers had seven other top-five team finishes at NCAA Championship events.[27]

As an undergrad at Purdue, Voinoff was one of the stars of Purdue football's first real golden era, starting for three years at tackle and helping the team to Big Ten titles in 1929 and 1931. It turned out Voinoff was a pretty good golf coach for a football player. He retired in 1975, handing the golf program over to one of his star pupils, Joe Campbell. Voinoff continued to play golf daily and eventually moved south to Florida. He died late in 1989 in Cape Coral, Fla. He was 82 years old.[28]

Several others helped out Burnham and his staff throughout the 1943 season as athletics was a bit of an all-hands-on-deck venture at the time. Those part-time football staffers included Claude Reeck, Ward "Piggy" Lambert and Guy "Red" Mackey. All three had filled in in when they could by serving as an extra body at practice from time to time while also helping out with scouting future opponents. Of course, all three were in the middle of all-time Hall of Fame careers in other areas.

Mackey was early in his tenure as the athletics director but before he was done, he would go down as one of the real legends in Purdue Athletics history. After playing end for the Boilermakers for three years in the late 1920s, Mackey moved right into coaching after graduation. He spent more than a decade on the coaching staff before being named athletics director in 1941, a post he would hold for three decades, until his death in 1971.[29] During his tenure, Mackey shepherded the department into the modern era of collegiate athletics. He helped found the department's fundraising arm, the John Purdue Club, oversaw five different renovations of Ross-Ade Stadium, and the creation of a new basketball arena later named in his memory.[30]

While Mackey was at the beginning of his tenure leading the Boilermakers in 1943, Piggy Lambert was nearing the end of his legendary run in West Lafayette. Lambert began his coaching career at Purdue in 1916, leading the basketball and baseball programs.[31] After taking a year off to serve in WWI, Lambert returned to campus and coached for the next 28 years. On the hardwood he won 371 games, 11 Big Ten titles and the 1932 Helms Foundation National Championship. He coached 16 All-Americans including 1932 National Player of the Year John Wooden.[32] He also won 163 games with the baseball team and saw several former players reach the major leagues.[33] Lambert retired from Purdue following the 1946 seasons to become the commissioner for the National Basketball League. Lambert held that position for three years, playing an integral role in the league's merger with the Basketball Association of America, leading to the creation of the modern NBA.[34]

Claude Reeck didn't have quite as much success leading the Purdue wrestling team as Lambert did on the hardwood, but it was close. Reeck coached the grapplers from 1936 to 1969.[35] In that span, he led six teams to Big Ten titles and three individuals to NCAA titles.[36] He also coached 21 All-Americans and led the Boilermakers to six Top Ten NCAA finishes as a team.[37] In 1959, Reeck coached the Team USA to a resounding victory at the Pan Am Games, where his wrestlers took the title in every weight class contested.[38]

It was quite a collection of talent on the sidelines for the Boilermakers in 1943. Every member of the coaching staff except

Burnham and Dienhart are members of the Purdue Intercollegiate Athletics Hall of Fame. Of course, the best coaching in the world doesn't matter if you don't have talent on the field. The 1943 Boilermakers certainly had that. And for a lot of them, the greatness they achieved during the '43 season was only the beginning.

CHAPTER 17

AFTER THE SEASON: THE PLAYERS

The 1944 Boilermakers had a number of familiar names on the squad returning to play for Coach Cecil Isbell. Among them were '43 regulars Babe Dimancheff, Stan Dubicki and Frank Bauman along with key reserves Tom Hughes and Bump Elliott. The team went 5-5 on the year with three of those losses coming to military institutions. The Boilermakers fell to Great Lakes to open the year, dropped a heartbreaker to Iowa Pre-Flight and were shut out by third-ranked Navy late in the season.[1]

Of course, with the war still on and Purdue still a participant in the V-12 program, the coaching staff had to once again figure out the roster on the fly. On October 30, another round of V-12 trainees was called to active duty and Isbell lost the services of Bauman, Dubicki, Elliott and Walt Poremba.[2] All four men headed to Parris Island with their V-12 class, just as their teammates had done 12 months earlier. Dimancheff took over the team's captaincy from Bauman and the squad that remained pressed on once more.

The year wasn't without some serious high points. Bauman and Dimancheff were named first-team all-conference and Babe also took home first-team All-America honors.[3,4] As one of the few civilians on the Boilermaker squad, Dimancheff provided a touch of stability for the team in that tumultuous time. The Indianapolis native rushed for 830 yards and totaled 12 touchdowns on the season, winning the conference scoring title. He was named the team's most valuable player for the season.[5] And he was one of a several players who went on to great success, both on and off the gridiron.

Dick Barwegen

Barwegen was a rarity on the 1943 team in that he was one of the few holdovers from the '42 season. The young man from Chicago's south side chose to attend Purdue after a legendary high school career at Fenger High School, where he helped the Titans to 37 straight wins and a city championship.[6] At Fenger, Barwegen anchored the front line that also included future Purdue teammate John Genis. Barwegen started for the Boilermakers in 1942 and was so good in the '43 season that he was named the team's most valuable player.

In the January 1944, Barwegen answered the call of the nation, joining the United States Army Enlisted Reserve Corps. He reported to Fort Sherridan in Lake County, Illinois, for training with the Army Air Force. Barwegen joined the Air Force for the duration of the war. While serving with both the 2nd Air Force and the 4th Air Force, he played on football teams comprised of fellow airmen.[7]

At the conclusion of the war, Barwegen returned to Purdue with a year of eligibility remaining as it had been determined that war-time years would not count against a player's eligibility from an NCAA standpoint. He stepped right back into a starring role on the front lines for the Boilermakers, earning first-team all-conference honors in 1946.

Barwegen had the distinction of being the only player to ever play for the College All-Star team four times, twice being elected captain for the squad put together to play an exhibition against the reigning NFL champion.[8] Of course, the war played a part in that, as did Purdue's proximity to Chicago, where the game was contested each August. Even more impressive was that Barwegen helped the team of collegians to victories over the professionals in three of those four games, including a 16-0 shutout over the reigning NFL champion Chicago Bears in 1947.

Barwegen was drafted by both the Boston Yanks in the National

Football League and the New York Yankees in the All-American Football Conference.[9] He ended up with the Yankees for the 1947 season, earning second-team All-AAFC honors, and was then sent to the Baltimore Colts as the league attempted to spread good players around to help the league stay relevant. It was in Baltimore where he reunited with head coach Cecil Isbell. When Isbell was hired by the Colts, he immediately targeted Barwegen as a player that would make the squad better.

"I wanted Barwegen on the team," Isbell said to the *Baltimore Sun* at the time. "He's a great lineman on offense and defense and he's a great competitor. You should never underestimate the lift a player like that can give a team."[10]

It paid off as Barwegen earned first-team All-AAFC honors with the Colts in 1948 and 1949 before he was on the move again.[11] This time it was Chicago Bears legend George Halas who had taken notice as he sent five players to Baltimore (including future Hall of Fame quarterback George Blanda) to acquire Barwegen.[12]

Now playing for his hometown Bears, Barwegen continued his own personal run of excellence. He earned consensus first-team NFL All-Pro honors in 1950 and 1951 and was named second-team All-Pro in 1952.[13] Following the 1952 season, he was traded back to Baltimore where he made his home in the offseason while running a successful seafood business. He played two more seasons with the Colts and spent a year in the Canadian Football League before retiring. Barwegen was named to the NFL's All-Decade team for the 1950s despite playing just half of the decade and his name routinely comes up when mentioning the greatest all-time players for both the Colts and the Bears.[14]

Barwegen coached a bit, then walked away from football entirely, entering the business world, eventually becoming a national sales representative with Glidden Corporation. In the fall of 1966, his life was cut short when, at the age of 44 he suffered a massive heart attack.[15]

Edward Cycenas

Ed Cycenas entered the 1943 season as one of the few known entities for Coach Burnham and company. An important piece on the 1942 club, he was one of the only holdovers for '43 squad. Unfortunately for him, his season ended before it really began as

Cycenas suffered a knee injury during fall training camp. Cycenas didn't get a chance to contribute to the perfect season on the field, though Burnham still valued his presence enough to include him on every travel roster for the season.

Cycenas shipped off to Parris Island a week before the rest of the Marines in late October, his season already long over. He matriculated through boot camp and then officers' training school before being deployed to the Pacific. In October 1945, on the morning of Purdue's Homecoming game against Iowa, a small dispatch was printed in the *Lafayette Journal & Courier.* Ensign Edward J. Cycenas had been officially declared dead by the Department of the Navy. No additional details were given.[16]

Lou DeFilippo

Dick Barwegen wasn't the only former Purdue lineman Isbell brought with him to Baltimore in the late 1940s. He also brought in Lou DeFilippo, albeit in a different capacity. Lou's playing days were over by the time Isbell took over the Colts organization so Cecil brought him in as an assistant coach.

DeFilippo stopped playing for the Boilermakers when they entered conference play but he didn't leave the program. Hanging around until the other V-12 men were activated in late October, Lou then shipped out also. On a different trajectory than the Marines on the squad, DeFilippo was a Navy man and, after joining the SeaBees, was shipped to Camp Peary, Virginia. He actually played football in 1944 for Camp Peary alongside several other former NFL players, before being deployed to the Philippines.[17]

After the war, DeFilippo returned the New York Giants for three seasons, resuming his pro career that had been interrupted to join the Navy and fight the Japanese. He spent a year on Isbell's staff then spent a few years on the coaching staffs Fordham and Columbia before settling into a fine career as a very successful high school coach.[18] DeFilippo coached at East Meadow High School on Long Island then moved to Derby High School in New Haven, Conn. His first two teams at Derby High went undefeated winning 19 games in a row. By the time he retired in 1982, DeFilippo run up a total of 116 wins at the school including five perfect seasons.[19]

DeFilippo's career accolades included being named the National

Football Foundation's Coach of the Year as well as induction into the Fordham Athletics Hall of Fame and the Connecticut High School Coaches Association Hall of Fame. After he retired, the field at Derby High School was named in his honor.

DeFilippo died on March 5, 2000, at age 83 while wintering in Miami with his wife, Agnes.

The DeFilippo legacy carried on at Purdue as well when, in 1962, his son Lou DeFilippo, Jr. elected to be a Boilermaker. Lou, Jr., started for three seasons for Jack Mollenkopf's teams, playing in 1962, 1964 and 1965 alongside Purdue legend Bob Griese.[20] Ironically, Lou, Jr., was born in November 1943, just a month after his dad played his final game at Purdue.

Boris "Babe" Dimancheff

By the end of the 1944 season, Dimancheff was the only regular remaining from the 1943 Boilermaker squad. He came to Purdue with two years of eligibility left and certainly made the most of his time in West Lafayette. After playing in the East-West Shrine Game for college all-stars, Dimancheff was drafted by the Boston Yanks of the National Football League.[21]

After two years in Boston, Dimancheff was traded to the Chicago Cardinals. He played for the Cardinals at Comiskey Park for three seasons, helping them to capture the 1947 NFL Championship while finishing as runners-up in the 1948 season. Dimancheff closed out his NFL career with the crosstown Chicago Bears in 1952. All told, in seven seasons of pro football, Babe accumulated nearly 2,000 total yards and scored 15 touchdowns.[22]

His playing career over, Dimancheff wasted no time moving on to the next chapter of his life on the sidelines. And, oddly enough, he followed a very familiar trajectory. Dimancheff spent a year on the sidelines at Butler, his original school. He then spent a year as an assistant freshman coach at Purdue. In 1954, Dimancheff took the coaching job at Hamtramck High School near Detroit. He led the Maroons to two Michigan state titles in his three seasons at the helm. Then, once again, the NFL beckoned.

In 1957, Babe got a call from Buddy Parker, his former coach with the Chicago Cardinals who asked Dimancheff to join the staff of his new team. Dimancheff coached the defensive backfield for the Pittsburgh Steelers for three seasons then joined the expansion Dallas

Cowboys staff for two years, coaching under the soon-to-be legendary Tom Landry. Dimancheff later made coaching stops at Wake Forest and with the upstart United Football League. He then reunited with another former coach, spending six seasons in the staff with of George Halas's Chicago Bears teams from 1966-1972. After seven seasons in Chicago, Dimancheff took a job in Anaheim as the offensive coordinator with the Southern California Sun of the World Football League. When the league folded, Dimancheff stayed in the Los Angeles area. But after a coaching career that lasted more than two decades and saw him experience success at every level, Dimancheff retired from the game of football.[23]

Dimancheff was elected to the Indiana Football Hall of Fame in 2007 shortly before passing at the age of 86. In 2009, he was posthumously enshrined in the Purdue Athletics Hall of Fame as well.

Stanley Dubicki

Stan Dubicki was a V-12 transfer from tiny Shurtleff College in Alton, Ill., where the South Bend native starred at halfback in 1942. When he transferred to Purdue, it didn't take long for Dubicki to carve out a spot in the Boilermaker backfield as well, despite being a bit smaller than most of his counterparts. After making a big impact in 1943, he helped lead a talented backfield for most of 1944 as well before shipping out mid-season along with Bauman, Elliott and a handful of others.

Training lasted nearly as long as the war so by the time Dubicki was deployed, Hawaii was as far as he got. He served out his time in the Marines, then returned to Purdue where he earned his degree in 1949. Stan and his bride Esther returned to South Bend. He didn't play football anymore after the war. Instead, he got his competitive juices flowing by competing in regular bowling leagues and was a regular in the South Bend City Golf Championship well into his 60s.

The Dubicki's retired to Orange Park, Fla., in 1999 and he died peacefully of natural causes 13 years later at age 91.[24]

Chalmers "Bump" Elliott

Bump Elliott was a late season replacement for Purdue in 1943 as he had to put in his first semester of military training before gaining eligibility as a true freshman. But he made his mark in those final two games of '43, with interceptions against Minnesota and Indiana. He was one of the stars of the 1944 team before being called to active duty in late October, missing the final four games of the season.

Elliott was part of the fourth wave of V-12 trainees to be activated and by the time he and his class were finished with basic training on Parris Island and officers school, first at Camp LeJuene, N.C and then at Quantico, Va., hostilities were nearly over in the Pacific. In fact, V-J Day occurred while Elliott was en route from Virginia to San Diego, the final stop before heading across the Pacific.

Elliott and his unit continued on to Hawaii and then spent nearly a year in China helping with the post-war efforts before his service ended. With two years of college remaining, Elliott considered returning to Purdue to finish as a Boilermaker. However, while he was overseas, his fiancée Barbara had graduated from Purdue and the football program had a dramatically different look with new coaches and very few players he was familiar with. Untethered to Purdue, Elliott decided to join his younger brother Pete at the University of Michigan, the school he had been sent to three years earlier as a V-12 trainee.

As a Boilermaker, Bump Elliott had shown a lot of promise. As a Wolverine, he far surpassed anyone's expectations. Elliott hadn't been on American soil much more than a week before he solidified his starting role in the Michigan backfield. Michigan finished 6-2-1 that season and ranked sixth in the nation. In 1947, Elliott helped the Wolverines to a perfect 10-0 record capped off by a 49-0 demolishing of USC in the Rose Bowl. Michigan shared the national title with Notre Dame and Elliott earned All-America honors as well as the vaunted *Chicago Tribune's* Big Ten MVP award.[25] Following the season, Elliott was drafted by the Detroit Lions but passed on a career in the NFL to become a coach instead.

Bump and Pete headed to Oregon State University to work for two seasons as assistants with the Beavers. The brothers finally parted ways in 1952 when Bump headed to the University of Iowa as the backfield coach for the Hawkeyes, a post he held for five seasons. He left Iowa City to join the staff at his alma mater and after two years of coaching the Wolverines backfield, Elliott was elevated to the head job for Michigan.[26]

Elliott coached at Michigan for a decade, logging a 51-42-2 record that included the 1964 Big Ten title and a Rose Bowl victory.

Incidentally, younger brother Pete was named the head coach at the University of Illinois in 1960 and the two faced off, on opposing sidelines, for seven seasons. Big brother had a decided advantage in those matchups, posting a 6-1 record against his younger sibling, including being the only blemish on Illinois' record in 1963 when the Fighting Illini went 8-1-1 and won the Rose Bowl with team MVP Dick Butkus.[27]

After calling it quits on the sideline following the 1968 season, Bump Elliott spent two seasons as an associate athletics director at Michigan before the Hawkeyes came calling once more. His mentor during his time at Iowa, Forest Evashevski, was retiring from his post as the athletics director and Elliott, it was determined, was well-suited for the job. For the next two decades, Bump Elliott would revolutionize athletics at the University of Iowa.

During his 21 years at the helm, Iowa teams won a combined 41 Big Ten titles across six different sports.[28] He made the decision in 1976 to hire Dan Gable to take over the already successful wrestling program and Gable turned Iowa Wrestling into one of the great dynasties in the history of college sports, winning 16 NCAA titles in the next 21 years.[29] Elliott also hired Hall of Fame coaches Hayden Fry for the football program, Lute Olson and Dr. Tom Davis for the men's basketball team and C. Vivian Stringer for the women's basketball team. Fry led the Hawkeyes to four conference titles and 17 consecutive winning seasons.[30] Olson and Stringer both led Iowa to Final Four appearances while on campus and Davis retired as the program's all-time leader in wins.[31]

Elliott also oversaw the construction of Carver-Hawkeye Arena, several renovations of Kinnick Stadium and shepherded Iowa into the modern era of collegiate sports. After 21 years at the helm for the Hawkeyes, Elliott retired in 1991 as the longest-tenured athletics director in school history, a distinction he still holds. Bump and his wife Barbara remained in Iowa City after retirement, having made that community their home until his passing in 2019 at the age of 94.[32]

Tom Hughes

Tom Hughes came to Purdue from Missouri and was a reserve tackle in 1943, taking over kicking duties late in the season as well. By the 1944 season, he was a mainstay of the Boilermakers' front wall.

After a short stint in the Marines, Hughes returned to West Lafayette to finish out his college career as a Boilermaker. It worked out pretty well for him. In 1945, Hughes and the Boilermakers opened the season with five straight wins and rose to as high as #4 in the AP poll before closing out the campaign at 7-3 overall. Hughes earned first-team All-America honors and in the spring of 1946 was awarded the Big Ten Medal of Honor, an award based on academic and athletic achievement.[33] Like Elliott, Hughes also passed up a pro career and turned to coaching. From 1946 to 1950, Hughes was an assistant football and baseball coach at the University of Oregon. Hughes also spent time on the staffs at Purdue and North Dakota at the college ranks and with the Baltimore Colts and the New York Yankees at the pro level.

In 1956, Hughes was hired as the head coach for the University of California-Santa Barbara football program. However, he resigned after less than a year on the job citing health issues. Hughes stayed in California and went into the insurance business. In March 1980, Hughes suffered massive heart attack and passed at age 60.[34]

William "Pinky" Newell

Pinky Newell was a little-used, 150-pound reserve on the 1943 Boilermaker team but by the end of his career, he probably had as big an impact on Purdue Athletics as anyone associated with the team. Newell lettered just one year with the Boilermakers and shipped off to the Pacific in early 1944, a first lieutenant in the Marines. After the war, Newell returned to campus and completed his physical education degree in 1947. He then did an intensive year of study at Stanford University and was awarded his certificate in physical therapy in 1948, becoming a physical trainer.

Newell spent a year as the head trainer at Washington State before returning to Purdue for that same position in 1950. In 1955, he helped to create the National Athletic Trainers Association and served on the board for more than a decade.[35] Newell was the head athletic trainer for Purdue Athletics for 28 years, where he worked hand-in-hand with former teammate and one-time foe, Purdue team physician Dr. Bill Combs, then spent another six years as the university's chief physical therapist at the student health center. Newell was also an assistant professor in the physical education department at Purdue.[36]

Highly respected and intensely sought after, Newell was the athletic trainer for the College All-Star football game several times and was a trainer for the United States Olympic team in 1976, 1980 and 1984. He was also one of four host trainers at the 1984 Summer Olympics in Los Angeles, duties that he wrapped up just weeks before his death in October of that year.[37]

Keith Parker

Keith Parker also came to Purdue from Missouri and was expected to play a big role with the Boilermakers before the injuries slowed his development. He returned in time to join Vacanti and Dimancheff in the starting backfield for the Indiana game. After deploying with the Marines, Parker returned home to the St. Louis area, settling on the Illinois side of the Mississippi River in Granite City.

Parker became a teacher and coach at Granite City High School and Coolidge Junior High. But it was as an official that Parker found his true calling. For more than three decades, Parker distinguished himself as among the top high school basketball and football officials in the state of Illinois, earning the distinction as the Illinois Boys Basketball Official of the Year in 1988. He was also inducted into the National High School Sports Hall of Fame in 1990.[38]

Parker remained in Granite City until his death in 2007. He was 84 years old.

Bernard Tetek

Unlike a lot of his former teammates who used football as a vocation, either as a player, coach or referee, Bernie Tetek used the game as a means to an end for his life's work: the law. Tetek came to Purdue after playing at Tulane in 1942. He did his stint in the Marines, was wounded in battle earning a Purple Heart, and then returned to the state of Indiana to attend law school at Valparaiso.[39] Tetek played football for the Crusaders while earning his law degree and, upon graduation, the Gary, Ind., native stayed in his home region in Northwest Indiana.

Tetek had a 40-year career as a litigator, arguing numerous cases before the Indiana Supreme Court.

Sam Vacanti

If Tony Butkovich was the engine that made Elmer Burnham's T-formation offense work, Sam Vacanti was the ignition that put everything into motion. The Omaha, Neb., native ran the same offense in his first two years of college ball at the University of Iowa and then excelled in the spotlight for the Boilermakers in 1943. The Marine trainee was on a different training schedule that Butkovich, Agase and the rest so he was able to finish out the '43 season and didn't get his call to active duty until late June 1944 along with Mike Kasap, Joe Buscemi and the second wave of V-12 trainees.

Vacanti headed to Parris Island and then the Pacific before returning to Nebraska after the war. With eligibility remaining, Vacanti elected to enroll at the University of Nebraska to compete for his third collegiate program in five years.[40] Vacanti earned the starting quarterback spot and played both ways just as he had at Purdue, his elite athleticism making him an even better defensive back than he was a quarterback. "Slinging Sammy" as he became known earned second-team all-conference honors despite the Cornhuskers finishing with a 3-6 record.[41]

Vacanti was drafted by the Chicago Rockets of the All-American Football Conference in 1947 and started for them in '47 and '48. The Rockets were miserably bad, posting 1-13 records in back to back seasons during his time there. However, those two wins both came against the Baltimore Colts, and head coach Cecil Isbell had seen enough of his former pupil that he wanted to bring him on board. The Colts traded for Vacanti during the 1948 season and in 1949 he split time with future Hall of Fame signal caller Y.A. Tittle.[42]

Vacanti's pro football career was cut short when the Marines came calling once again in late 1949. Vacanti was called back to active duty, serving in the Korean War and eventually attaining the rank of Major.[43] Following his second stint serving Uncle Sam, Vacanti returned to Omaha where he became a teacher and coach, served as the Nebraska State Athletics Commissioner and eventually served for four years on the Omaha City Council.[44] In late 1981, Vacanti suffered a heart attack while visiting the Omaha chapter of the 40 and 8 Club, a private veteran's group associated with the American Legion. He was 59 years old.[45]

CHAPTER 18

AFTER THE SEASON: THE PURD-ILLINI

Clearly the team most negatively affected by the V-12 transfers was the University of Illinois. The Fighting Illini lost several starters to the program, the bulk of them ending up at Purdue. Illinois players set the foundation of Purdue's greatness with two former Fighting Illini earning All-American honors in West Lafayette (Alex Agase and Tony Butkovich) while six former Illini players earned all-conference honors. It was a bitter pill for Illinois head coach Ray Eliot to swallow, watching his former players win the conference crown while his current players finished the season 3-7. Coach Eliot would have his glory…he'd just have to wait a few years.

Agase, Mike Kasap, John Genis and all the rest would deploy overseas and serve their country. But by early 1946, with the war over and their enlistments coming to an end, all had eligibility remaining and needed some classes to earn their degrees. In April of that year, Genis, Kasap and Agase drove to the central Illinois campus to pledge their loyalty to the Fighting Illini and vow a return in the fall.[1] They had the option of returning to Purdue and, although they enjoyed the Boilermaker experience quite a lot, these Illinois natives wanted to return to their state's flagship institution.

When the team opened the 1946 season with a 33-7 win over Pittsburgh, there was a familiar feel to the front line. Agase held down the right guard spot with Kasap at the left tackle and Frank Bauman at right end. Genis and Joe Buscemi both missed the game due to injury but would return by midseason. After starting the year 2-2 with losses to Notre Dame and Indiana, Illinois went on a tear.

The highlight of the Big Ten slate was played on October 5 during the Big Ten opener when the Fighting Illini welcomed Purdue to Memorial Stadium. It wasn't a particularly good game as the Illinois squad routed the Boilermakers by a score of 43-7, their first win in the series since 1919. The best part of the afternoon, for both sides, was what happened after.

Agase, Kasap, Genis and Bauman headed over to the Purdue sidelines to visit with some of their former teammates, including Dick Barwegen and Tony Lehmkuhl. There weren't a lot of holdovers from the 1943 team but those who were still around shared a few words with their buddies.[2] Eventually, Joe Dienhart and Red Mackey joined the group. After a few minutes, Agase asked, "Where's Cecil?"[3]

"He went over to congratulate Ray Eliot on the win," replied Mackey.[4]

Agase jogged across the field trying to find his old coach but quickly surmised that he had missed Isbell and came back to the group.

"He's already gone," Agase reported. "Let's go to the Purdue dressing room and find him."[5]

Isbell was, in fact, in the visitor's locker room by then, meeting with reporters to talk about his team's dismal day on the field. Staring a hole through the floor, Isbell answered a few questions about the game and was finally asked about his former players suiting up on the other side.

"They were good ball players then," said Isbell, continuing to sullenly stare downward. "They're still mighty good ball players."[6]

Suddenly, Agase burst into the Purdue dressing room, Kasap close behind. Isbell's face lit up.

"I didn't get a chance to see you before," Agase said. "It was a good game...a real clean game all around." The two men grinned and shook hands and Isbell turned to Kasap.[7]

"Nice game, Mike, a real swell game," Isbell said to a silent Kasap. The men stood there for a few minutes more catching up, Agase not missing a chance to pass along a small scouting report on Purdue's next opponent, a Notre Dame team that had beaten Illinois just the week before.[8] While it was a bad day for the Purdue football squad, it was a great scene to behold and very reminiscent what had happened three years earlier in West Lafayette.

A few moments later, while still talking with the media, Agase felt the need to go on the record about his feelings about Purdue. "We all were treated swell at Purdue, and anyone that writes anything about discord is nuts," Agase said. "We wish nothing but the best for Guy Mackey and everyone else down there."[9]

The Fighting Illini ball club won their final five games of the regular season to finish with an 8-2 record, 6-1 in conference, and the outright Big Ten title. On January 1, 1947, fifth-ranked Illinois took on fourth-ranked UCLA in the 33rd Annual Rose Bowl, the first to be played under the new agreement between the Pacific Coast Conference and the Big 9 (later the Pac-12 and the Big Ten). Thanks to a dominant performance by the front line, Illinois handled the Bruins easily in a 45-14 win. The Fighting Illini rushed for 320 yards and completely dominated on defense, forcing six UCLA turnovers and returning a pair of interceptions for scores in the fourth quarter.[10]

Coach Ray Eliot and the Fighting Illini faithful finally got a chance to see how good those Purd-Illini players could be. Eliot would coach the Illini for another 13 years, winning two more Big Ten titles and another Rose Bowl in 1951.[11] Following the 1946 season, Agase once again earned consensus All-America honors and was also named the 1946 Big Ten MVP by the *Chicago Tribune*. Ten Illini players earned all-conference honors, including Agase and Kasap.[12] It was a year for the ages at Illinois, even if they had to defer satisfaction for a few years.

John Genis

Genis was part of the first wave of V-12 trainees to head to Parris Island, playing his final game with the Boilermakers on that special afternoon at Wisconsin. Part of the 29th Marine Regiment, Sixth Marine Division along with Butkovich, Genis headed to the Pacific on August 1, 1944 and soon arrived on Guadalcanal in the southern Solomon Islands.[13] The unit spent the next several months building up a base while doing intensive training in the rugged terrain, preparing for the next step in the march toward Japan. On Christmas Eve, Genis joined Butkovich and a team of fellow Marines from the 29th in a football game against the 4th Marine Regiment.[14] The game, later dubbed the "Mosquito Bowl" for its tropical location, came about like many athletic contests through the years…because a few men were sitting around talking over a beer or two. Beers led to bragging and that, naturally, led to a wager over which regiment had the more impressive football talent.[15]

Both certainly had a case to make. In addition to Butkovich and Genis, the 29th boasted a few players from Notre Dame, at least one each from Wisconsin, Duke, Mississippi and TCU as well as a former member of the Detroit Lions. The 4th, meanwhile, had an All-American of its own in Wisconsin end Dave Schreiner as well as players from Michigan State, Fordham and Notre Dame. Also included were a handful of former pros and another former Boilermaker, Bruce Warren from the 1942 Purdue squad.[16]

It was decided the game would take place on the parade grounds of the 29th Regiment's base. On Christmas Eve 1944, an estimated 10,000 Marines showed up to watch this top-flight entertainment, with many no doubt making their own wagers along the way. Of the parade grounds, Genis would later point out the conditions were less than ideal.

"It wasn't any better than an alley on Chicago's South Side," he said.[17]

With no protective gear and lousy ground on which to play, rules specified a basic two-hand touch game, barring tackling and hoping to save both sides from injuries. Of course, those rules lasted until the end of the first series of plays and eventually the game devolved into a full-contact, all-out battle. When the dust settled, every gambler went home unhappy as the final score was 0-0. After the game, Genis mailed a copy of the game program from the "Mosquito Bowl" to Coach Eliot back at Illinois.[18]

Four months later, both regiments were on their way to Okinawa for what would be the next battle as the Allied forces continued to hop scotch their way toward mainland Japan. It would be the first full engagement for Genis and many in the 29th as they had joined the regiment after its most recent engagement at Saipan in July.

The 29th was initially set to be a reserve force on April 1, 1945, when the Marines landed on Okinawa's western shore but they were able to come ashore due a complete lack of Japanese resistance to the landing.[19] It would not be a sign of things to come. For the next ten weeks, the 29th faced intense action on the small but vitally important island. Just 415 miles from mainland Japan, taking control of Okinawa would allow a forward staging area for both aerial attacks on Japan and the what was expected to be the needed ground assault on the island nation to ultimately end the war. Both sides knew of the island's importance and the fighting was fierce.

In June, Genis and the rest of the 29th regiment were sent to Guam, replaced on the battlefield by the 8th Marines. Genis was among those being treated for shell shock after a mortar round exploded just feet away from him.[20] The 29th had moved to Saipan by early August and were there on V-J Day when the Japanese surrendered.[21] Genis and the rest of the 6th Marines headed to China to help in the postwar stabilization efforts and the repatriation of Japanese forces to their home country after their surrender.[22]

Genis returned stateside and enrolled at the University of Illinois in time for the 1946 summer session.[23] He decided to try playing his way back into shape through a very competitive intramural summer softball league on campus while taking classes. After leading his team to the summer championship, Genis joined the rest of the Purd-Illini fellas for football practice in mid-August. Unfortunately, he injured his knee near the end of fall camp and missed a good portion of the season, returning just in time to play in the Rose Bowl.

Genis graduated in June and signed a contract with the Baltimore Colts but elected to forego a chance at the professional ranks, returning his $6,000 signing bonus and choosing to stay on campus to continue rehabilitating his knee injury instead.[24] Genis, married and with a newborn daughter, entered graduate school instead, hoping to wait for a good coaching offer to come along. Instead, he completed his graduate schooling and saw his career take a distinct turn.

Post-war America in the late 40s provided a unique opportunity for former military officers. During the war, the FBI had more than tripled in size to combat domestic spying and other crimes. And even though the hostilities had ended, the threats to America had not, especially as the country moved into the Cold War era for the next five decades. Genis took advantage of this need and joined the FBI, spending the next several decades with the Bureau.[25]

Genis lived until 2002, passing in mid-January of that year in Fort Myers, Fla. He was laid to rest in Arlington National Cemetery.

Mike Kasap

Genis's line mate was a year younger than most of the other Purd-Illini players and, as such, was not called to active duty in November 1943. He was allowed to finish out the season with the Boilermakers before heading to Parris Island in late June 1944. After basic training in South Carolina, he was sent to officer's school at Quantico, Va., and then Camp Pendleton, Calif. Lieutenant Kasap was granted a leave in early August 1945 and returned to Champaign to take in a preseason Fighting Illini practice.[26]

Kasap was expecting to be deployed with the rest of his unit upon returning to California. However, with the war ending by the time he returned to Camp Pendleton, the need for massive troop deployments across the Pacific was vastly diminished. Just four months later, Kasap was discharged by the Marines.[27]

After spending the rest of the academic year back home in LaSalle, Ill., Kasap re-enrolled for the fall of 1946 and rejoined the Fighting Illini football squad.[28] Much like Genis, Kasap was dealt a blow via injury as a broken hand hampered his 1946 season. He, too, recovered in time to play in the Rose Bowl and then signed a pro contract, foregoing his final year of college eligibility. Kasap agreed to terms with the Cleveland Browns, to go play for former Ohio State head coach Paul Brown's new team in the All-American Football Conference.[29]

While Kasap didn't make the Browns roster, he did end up on Cecil Isbell's squad in Baltimore for the 1947 season, starting three games for the Colts.[30] In 1948, he became an assistant coach at the University of Vermont, citing the uncertainty of being a down-the-roster player in the professional ranks. While at Vermont, in addition to coaching the football lines he was also the school's hockey coach. After four years with the Catamounts, Kasap moved back closer to home, eventually teaching and coaching at his alma mater, LaSalle-Peru Township High School.[31]

Kasap retired from teaching and remained in his home town until his death in October 1994, just a month shy of his 72nd birthday.

Joe Buscemi

Kasap had company on his June 1944 call to active duty in fellow Purd-Illini player Joe Buscemi. The end from Rockford, Ill., was a very pleasant surprise for the Boilermakers in the 1943 season. His training and deployment schedule closely mirrored Kasap's in that Buscemi didn't deploy overseas until mid-1945, after the fighting had ceased. Once he returned to the states, he also returned to Illinois to play out his eligibility in 1946 and 1947.[32] Buscemi was a permanent fixture for the Fighting Illini those two years despite being undersized compared to others at the end position. And he was a winner. The combined record of the 1943 Purdue team and the 1946-47 Illinois teams was 22-5-1 with two Big Ten titles.

After graduation, Buscemi moved to Cincinnati where he lived until being activated once again by the Marines. In 1952, Captain Joe Buscemi served in Korea, eventually attaining the rank of Major before retiring from the service.[33]

Once out of the Marines, Buscemi returned to Ohio and owned his own food wholesale company in Cleveland, the State Fish Company. He eventually retired to Palm Beach Gardens, Florida, where he died on April 23, 2009.[34]

Frank Bauman

Buscemi's classmate and fellow end Frank Bauman was also able to finish out the 1943 season. Bauman was fortunate enough to play most of the '44 campaign with the Boilermakers too before getting called to active duty in November 1944, earning first-team all-conference honors for his efforts.[35] Bauman attained the rank of 2nd Lieutenant in the Marines while matriculating through Parris Island, Camp LeJuene and Quantico, but like Elliott, Buscemi and Kasap before him, Frank Bauman did not complete training before the war reached its conclusion. Unfortunately, the same could not be said for his older brother.

Bob Bauman was a towering young man from the south suburbs of Chicago just like his younger sibling and excelled at football as well. Bob played at Wisconsin from 1940-42, starting at tackle on the Badgers 1942 National Title team.[36] He joined the marines in early 1943 and deployed with the 4th Marines in time to take part in the Battle of Guam. Bob Bauman was on Guadalcanal in late 1944 and played in the Mosquito Bowl against Butkovich and Genis.[37] And he was part of the replacement regiment that relieved Genis' group on Okinawa where, on June 6, Bauman was killed in action.[38]

Younger brother Frank put in his time in the Marines and, once discharged, returned to their hometown of Harvey, Ill. There he became a teacher and a football and track coach at his alma mater of Thornton Township High School, incidentally also the alma mater of Cleveland Indian player/manager Lou Boudreau who had brought his ball club to West Lafayette for spring training in 1943-45.

Bauman had some outstanding teams at Thornton Township, winning the Illinois state championship during an undefeated 1965 season. That team was still being talked about decades later when the Chicago Tribune counted it as among the best high school football teams in the history of the state, noting that that 1965 squad beat all comers by three touchdowns that year.[39]

Bauman also spent time as the athletics director at Thornwood High School in neighboring South Holland, Ill. Bauman retired in 1983 after 35 years of service in the Thornton Township School District.[40]

Bauman remained in the Chicagoland area for the remainder of his life, passing in April 2013 at the age of 88.

Alex Agase

By any measure, Alex Agase was a star player for both the Fighting Illini and the Boilermakers. A three-time All-American, Agase is the only player in college football history to earn that honor at two different schools. It was only the beginning of a great legacy the young man from Evanston, Ill., was building for himself.

After shipping to Parris Island with Butkovich, Genis and the rest of the Boilermakers in late 1943, Agase was assigned to the 1st Marine Division, a group that had seen a lot of action in the Guadalcanal Campaign, and the intense battles of Cape Gloucester and Peleliu. Agase and his unit helped replenish the division after heavy losses on Peleliu in late 1944. More than 1,200 Marines were killed and another 5,000 were wounded in one of the bloodiest battles of the Pacific Theatre.[41]

For the 1st Marines, just like the 6th Marines and most other Allied forces in the Pacific, the next step was Okinawa. And the battle-hardened 1st Marines would once again be in the thick of it. On April

1, 1945, Agase and the 1st Marines joined Butkovich, Genis and the 6th Marines and, along with the 10th Army Division, launched their assault on the western shore of Okinawa in the second-largest Allied invasion force of the war, trailing only the invasion of Normandy 10 months earlier.[42] Shockingly, they faced no initial resistance and the assault operated ahead of schedule as the Allied forces dug in. It wouldn't last. Eventually, the Americans faced intense resistance from the Japanese forces, which had made the tactical decision to dig in on the high ground in the cliffs and mountains of the island rather than fighting the initial assault.

Over the course of the next five weeks, American forces advanced only 1,000 yards, suffering heavy casualties daily.[43] By mid-May, the Marines were finally getting a foothold with Agase right in the thick of the action, according to a tale relayed to the folks back home via the *Chicago Tribune*.

"His helmet had been knocked off and battered by a hand grenade and his dungarees were ventilated by holes made by shell fragments. But Marine Lt. Alex Agase...had not been wounded and he was grinning thru a set of front line whiskers after leading his platoon up a ridge in front of Shuri, key position in the Japanese line."[44]

Agase's luck wouldn't hold. In early June, Agase was amongst the wounded, shot in the shoulder and in the thigh, just above the knee.[45] He was treated on the battlefield and then evacuated to a hospital in Guam to recover, writing home to his parents in Evanston that the wounds weren't all that serious and that he was eager to rejoin the fight.[46] Both gunshot wounds avoided making contact with any bones, cutting down on possible complications and recovery time. Agase was en route back to Okinawa when the island was finally captured on June 22.

After wrapping up the final duties of securing the island and the victory, Agase and the rest of the 1st Marine Division would turn their attention toward training for the next, and likely final, target: mainland Japan. However, that would quickly become unnecessary as, on August 6, the American B-29 bomber *Enola Gay* dropped an atomic bomb on Hiroshima, causing destruction never before seen in human history. Three days later, American B-29 *Bockscar* dropped a second atomic bomb over Nagasaki, effectively ending the war in the Pacific. Within a week, Emperor Hirohito issued a public statement surrendering.

Agase joined American forces in Japan to help negotiate the postwar peace, the dissolution of the Japanese fighting forces and the transfer of power. However, by the end of the year, he had returned home and, by the spring of 1946, was considering his future. In April he made a trip back to the University of Illinois to declare he would be with the Fighting Illini in the fall, joining his little brother Lou and the rest of his former teammates.

Agase had a great 1946 campaign, earning the *Chicago Tribune's* Silver Football as the player of the year in the Big Ten conference.[47] He was signed by the Los Angeles Dons in the All-American Football Conference in 1947 but was traded to the Chicago Rockets midway through his rookie year.[48] After finishing the season with the Rockets, Agase was shipped to the Cleveland Browns, the defending league champion. He hit his stride under head coach Paul Brown, helping Cleveland win two more AAFC titles in 1948 and 1949 before the franchise joined the National Football League in time for the 1950 season.[49]

With a talented team featuring several future Hall of Famers including Otto Graham, Lou Groza and Marion Motley, the Browns won the NFL Championship in 1950 and reached the championship game in 1951 before falling to the L.A. Rams.[50.] Agase was traded to the expansion Dallas Texans prior to the 1952 season but decided to call it a career and make a move into coaching. He signed on to be the line coach for the Texans under Jim Phelan, the former Purdue head man.[51] He played for the Baltimore Colts in the 1953 season, after the Texans disbanded, but then retired for good and moved to the college coaching ranks. Agase spent two years as an assistant at Iowa State and then went to work with former Cleveland Browns teammate Ara Parseghian at Northwestern University, back home in Evanston.[52]

Agase rose to be Parseghian's top assistant and when Notre Dame came calling for Parseghian in 1964, Agase slid into the head coaching position at Northwestern.[53] He spent nine years coaching the Wildcats from 1964 to 1972, finishing second in the Big Ten on two occasions and earning national coach of the year honors in 1970.[54] Following the 1972 season, Agase got an opportunity he couldn't pass up when one of the schools on his short list of programs he would leave Northwestern for came calling. And so, in mid-December 1972, Agase agreed to become the head coach at Purdue University, his former home. He had loved living in West Lafayette, always remembered it fondly and believed the football program had great potential.[55]

In four years at Purdue, Agase's teams always finished just below .500 for the season but they also finished in the top half of the Big Ten three of four years.[56] That tenure also included wins over #2 Notre Dame in 1974 and #1 Michigan in 1976, his final season at Purdue. He had 20 Purdue players drafted into the NFL, including three first-round picks and Carl Capria, Larry Burton and Ken Novak each earned All-America honors playing for Agase.[57]

After being let go following the 1976 season, Agase became the athletics director at Eastern Michigan in 1977, a post he held until 1982.[58] He spent five more years after that volunteering on Bo Schembechler's coaching staff at Michigan. Agase and Schembechler had worked together 25 years earlier on Parseghian's staff at Northwestern.

"Loving every minute of it," Agase said of returning to 15-hour days as a 60-year-old assistant coach. "I'm like a youngster at Christmas with a whole bunch of new toys."[59]

A 1963 inductee into the College Football Hall of Fame, Agase was selected in 1987 as a member of Purdue's All-Century team and in 1989 was chosen as a member of the Walter Camp Foundation's All-Century team.[60] A year later, he was named to the University of Illinois' All-Century team as well.[61]

In a 2001 interview with the *Lafayette Journal & Courier*, Agase talked about his time at Purdue and the things that stuck with him nearly six decades later.

"Football is teamwork and we jelled petty quickly," he said. "The coaches – Joe Dienhart, Sam Voinoff, Cecil Isbell and of course Elmer Burnham – did an excellent job of putting that team together. That's not easy to do, to take people who don't know each other, from various universities and get them to jell. But it was a talented team."[62]

Agase had an extra appreciation for the coaching job done by Burnham and company after spending several decades as a coach at the highest levels. He also said Dick Barwegen was as good a football player as he's ever seen. But the highest praise he saved for his old friend, Tony Butkovich.

"He was so tough," Agase said of Touchdown Tony. "He could run over you, he could make you miss, he could stiff arm. He had all the attributes of a great running back. He was strong, very competitive, and one great football player."[63]

Agase enjoyed retirement, watching a lot of football and staying involved with his church in his Florida gulf coast community. He passed away in 2007 at the age of 85.[64]

Agase was probably the best player on the 1943 Boilermaker squad, although the fact that it's up for debate shows just how talented that team was. But Butkovich was no doubt the star of the team, the engine that drove the record-setting offense and the individual for whom the team fought for on that historic October afternoon in Madison, earning the Big Ten scoring record. They couldn't have possibly known that day just how important that effort was and just how fleeting that joy would be.

CHAPTER 19

TOUCHDOWN TONY

When Tony Butkovich and the rest of the Purdue Marines headed to the Lafayette station to catch the train south to Parris Island, many of them would never return to campus. After all, they had been brought to Purdue for a very specific reason and now that part of their mission had been accomplished.

Butkovich had remained close with Genis and Agase throughout the entire process. The three had been close since their arrival in Champaign years earlier, spending time together on the gridiron and away from the field. In addition to being football teammates, all three were also on the Illinois baseball team in the spring of 1943 while Butkovich and Agase also wrestled for the Fighting Illini and Butkovich and Genis were fraternity brothers in the Delta Upsilon house. The three also roomed together at Purdue and so it made sense that they would ship off to boot camp together.[1]

Of course, Purdue wasn't the only football program that saw the 1943 season dramatically altered with just a few weeks to play. Thousands of V-12 trainees around the country received their orders to transfer on or before November 1. This included national powers like Notre Dame, Michigan and Southern California as well as smaller programs like the College of the Pacific and Colgate. Suddenly, Parris Island, S.C., had about the best collection of football talent of anywhere on the globe.

Never missing an opportunity to show national unity and garner support for the cause, the Navy's Office of Public Relations had several photo opportunities with the football heroes who were now in the Marines. One particular photo featured eleven former ball players lined up shoulder to shoulder as in a football formation. The starting lineup included Agase and Butkovich along with Heisman Trophy winner Angelo Bertelli from Notre Dame and All-American John Podesta from Pacific. The photo was taken near the end of boot camp and published in early January 1944 in newspapers from Racine, Wisc. to St. Petersburg, Fla.; Camden, N.J., to Oakland, Cali.[2]

Butkovich was the toast of the college football world and was involved in several different promotional photo opportunities before leaving Parris Island. When he did depart from basic training in early 1944, Butkovich headed to Camp LeJuene, N.C. with the rest of the 29th Marines and then to the west coast and the trip across the Pacific. In September, the 29th was assigned to the 6th Marine Division and headed to Guadalcanal to train for the Okinawa invasion.

Butkovich played in the "Mosquito Bowl" along with Genis on Christmas Eve, though even Touchdown Tony couldn't find the end zone on the 0-0 tie. Another way Butkovich passed the time on Guadalcanal was with correspondence back home and, in particular, to a very big fan. During the 1943 season, 8-year-old Tommy Milligan wrote a letter to his favorite football player asking for his autograph. The boy from Richmond, Ind., idolized Butkovich so when his response arrived with an autograph days later, it quickly became a prized possession.[3]

But even better than the autograph was the friendship that bloomed. The two continued to write letters even after Butkovich was no longer scoring touchdowns for the Boilermakers. They continued through Butkovich's officers' training and overseas deployment. One of Butkovich's letters actually arrived in Richmond when a Navy Seabee named Bill Keesling was home on leave and carried the letter in his shirt pocket from Guadalcanal to his east central Indiana hometown.[4] In one letter, Butkovich included a picture from the Mosquito Bowl and a detailed description of the game. In another letter, Butkovich vowed to make his way to Richmond whenever he returned from the war to meet his friend face to face.[5]

Butkovich went about his days training for the April 1, 1945 launch day. As a mortar man in the 3rd Battalion, 29th Regiment, he would be in the initial wave of the attack. In early April, Tony sent a letter back to the University of Illinois where his brother Bill continued carrying on the family name for the Illini. In the letter, written on a Japanese post card, Tony mentioned that he had celebrated his birthday on Okinawa on April 4.

"It's a helluva place to have a birthday," the now 24-year-old Butkovich wrote. "Sleeping in a fox hole, eating K and C rations."[6]

Butkovich's 29th Regiment made its way north on Okinawa, headed for the northwestern-facing Motobu Peninsula. They faced virtually no resistance along the route and made good progress, reaching the peninsula within a week of landing on Okinawa. As they explored Motobu, trying to get a fixed location on the enemy, there was only occasional resistance. Then the fighting commenced. Japanese forces were dug in on the higher ground of Mt. Yae-Take, a 1,200-foot peak in the center of the peninsula. The three divisions of the 29th Marines were split up into three columns to form multiple points of attack. Butkovich's 3rd Battalion was on the southern front and encountered heavy resistance along with roads made impassable due to mines and road blocks. The once lighting fast Marine advance ground to a halt.[7]

Japanese military forces had long used Okinawa as a training ground so they had an intimate knowledge of the terrain and knew just where the strengths and weaknesses of the island were. This likely explained why American forces faced no initial resistance as the Japanese knew they had a distinct advantage if they simply waited for American troops to approach their trap.[8]

As the battled progressed, Butkovich's 3rd Battalion was on the western front of the assault, attached to the 4th Marines, and his mortar units were dug in, sending a steady barrage of explosives up the slopes, trying to damage the Japanese defenses enough to aid the approach of ground forces. Intelligence now showed that there were likely more than 1,500 Japanese forces atop Mt. Yae-Take with the hilly and broken terrain making the approach exceedingly difficult.[9]

After a week of heavy fighting with little to show for it, American forces changed tactics, electing to triangulate their fronts in the assault on Mt. Yae-Take, forcing the enemy into a single defensive position. The Americans would then rely on heavy artillery and air strikes to overcome the Japanese defenses.[10] The new approach worked and on April 17th, the Battle of Yae-Take was nearly won by American forces. Two companies of the 4th Marine Division occupied the summit of the mountain while the 29th Regiment dug in just short of the objective and the enemy was in retreat, switching to guerilla tactics rather than their more traditionally organized defense.[11]

Late in the evening, Butkovich and his unit found a place to settle for the night. According to Marine combat correspondent Sgt. Harold T Bolan, circumstances led them to eschew what would normally be precautionary measures.

"The battalion had picked a spot in the hills to rest before advancing the next morning," Sgt. Bolan wrote. "Since they'd soon be on the move again, most of the men lay on the ground without digging in. At 0200 (2 a.m.) there was a noise in the area. Butkovich raised up to investigate. He was shot through the chest, just above the heart."[12]

A sniper, under cover of darkness and at some distance, had killed Butkovich in an instant. The young man from St. David, Ill., so vibrant and full of life that his battalion mates had taken to calling him "Rugged Buck", was gone.[13]

"The battalion had suffered casualties before," continued Bolan's report. "Lots of good buddies were gone. But this morning gloom reached new depths, for Rugged Buck had been killed."[14]

"None of us can say anything nice enough about Buck," said his squad leader, Sgt. John Maskas, himself a former football player at the University of North Carolina.[15]

When the Battle of Yae-Take was over, more than 2,000 Japanese soldiers lay dead while American forces lost nearly a thousand men, including Corporal Anthony James Butkovich.[16] Fighting on Okinawa would continue for six more weeks with the final casualty figures on each side reaching staggering proportions. Japanese Imperial forces lost more than 110,000 while American forces lost more than 12,500 soldiers, Marines and sailors in what was the bloodiest battle in the Pacific.[17] It was also the final major engagement of the war.

Word was slow to reach the states, but once Butkovich's death was reported back home, there were newspaper headlines across the country. At the University of Illinois, his loss was particularly devastating.

"I'm dreadfully sorry to hear it," said Illinois coach Ray Eliot of his former player. "Not only was Tony a real American boy, but he was a fine and outstanding athlete. He was a very fine character and a fine fellow all around. He always gave an excellent account of himself. He was a real Fighting Illini."[18]

In his first column written after the publication of Butkovich's death, Lafayette Journal & Courier sports editor Gordon Graham wrote extensively about the one-time Boilermaker.

"We have been thinking for more than a week about the death of Tony Butkovich," Graham wrote on May 14. "Somehow we had the childish notion that nothing could kill that 190 pounds of football granite...but war takes its toll. After Tony and his Marine pals left Purdue, we were happy to read letters from the brilliant fullback in which he made clear statements that he would return to Purdue instead of Illinois after the war. How trivial that all seems now."[19]

Like thousands of other Americans who lost their lives fighting overseas, Butkovich was laid to rest at a military cemetery in Okinawa. He wouldn't be brought to his final resting place for four years. In 1946, Congress authorized the return of bodies to the United States at the government's expense.[20] More than 170,000 families chose this option, including the Butkovich family in St. David, Ill. In early June 1949, Corporal Tony Butkovich's body was returned home and laid to rest in Saint Mary's Cemetery in Canton, Ill.[21]

AFTERWORD

The 1943 Purdue Football team was unlike any other in the program's history, which stands to reason since it was a by-product of a challenge unlike any the United States had ever faced. Like Americans and American institutions everywhere, Purdue University rose to the challenge. And the war changed the university forever.

Enrollment at Purdue in the fall of 1940 was just under 7,000 students, nearly identical to the number of students in 1939.[1,2] By 1949, it had more than doubled to 14,200.[3] This was due in part to soldiers returning from war taking advantage of the GI Bill and enrolling in college. The enrollment figure in 1949 included 5,800 veterans but that figure was actually lower than the veteran enrollment from the previous two years.[4]

President Edward C. Elliott insisting that the university shift to a wartime mentality following the attack on Pearl Harbor had benefited not only the country but also the university itself. At the war's height, military personnel outnumbered civilian students two-to-one but, most importantly, the university itself remained vibrant. And with Elliott's leadership and involvement with various military committees, the long-term forecast for the university was bright.

Engineering continued to be the discipline that Purdue was most firmly grounded in and in the decade following the war's conclusion, Purdue engineers would be vital in laying the groundwork for the newly formed National Aeronautics and Space Administration. Purdue undergrads in the late 40s and early 50s included future NASA astronauts Gus Grissom, Roger Chaffee, Gene Cernan and Neil Armstrong.[5]

Between its inception in July 1943 and its termination in June 1946, the Navy's V-12 program saw over 125,000 enrollees and turned out more than 50,000 officers.[6] And the post-war accomplishments of V-12 trainees was nearly as impressive as what they did during the war. Thousands of Navy and Marine officers stayed in the military and made a career of it. Some 38 V-12 alums took their officers' commissions and rose to the rank of Admiral. Meanwhile, 15 V-12 Marines attained the field rank of General.

Former V-12 trainees also made their mark on American politics over the next several decades following the war. This group included ten U.S. Senators, nearly a dozen congressmen and four governors. This included figures that towered over the American landscape for decades, including Robert F. Kennedy, Daniel Patrick Moynihan, H. R. Haldeman, Pierre Salinger and Warren Christopher. More than two dozen V-12 men went on to become college and university presidents including future Purdue president Arthur G. Hansen. And the arts and entertainment world was blessed with several former trainees as well with the likes of Johnny Carson, Jack Lemmon, Sam Peckinpaugh and Roger Williams going on to have great careers in film and music.

Thousands more V-12 alums went on to work in various other industries and eventually rose to the top of such corporations as Boeing, Chase Manhattan Bank, Ford Motor Company, General Motors, Hershey Foods, Johnson and Johnson, Lockheed, Pfizer and Whirlpool, amongst many others.[7] Of the 131 schools involved, Purdue had amongst the largest V-12 enrollments, with more than 7,400 V-12 trainees coming to West Lafayette over the span of the program. This included 5,593 Naval officers and 1,859 Marines.[8]

For many of the members of the 1943 Boilermaker squad, Purdue would hold a special place in their hearts forever. Four decades later, several of them had a chance to show just how much. In the spring of 1983, Purdue held its annual Alumni Challenge Bowl where former players returned to take on the current Boilermaker squad. Although no members from the '43 team played, more than a dozen players returned to campus for the affair.

Those in attendance included John Genis, Mike Kasap, Frank Bauman, Keith Parker, James McMillen, Ed Gerker, Joe Morrow, Joe Hersch, Walt Poremba, Leonard Milauskas, Morris Kaastad, Pinky Newell and assistant coach Sam Voinoff. More players still joined the party six months later when they reconvened at the 1983 homecoming game including Lou DeFilippo. Alex Agase and Bump Elliott were unable to attend due to their duties at Iowa and Michigan, respectively.[9]

Newell spearheaded the reunion along with Voinoff, both of them having long resided in West Lafayette. One of the men in attendance was Leonard Milauskas, a civilian reserve on the Boilermaker squad. He recalled the reunion years later.

"I attended the 40th reunion and there were maybe 20 or so players there," Milauskas said. "It was interesting to talk to all of those guys about our exploits. I actually asked some of the guys if they knew what happened to Tony. That's when I found out he had been killed."[10]

Milauskas said he had followed the careers of Babe Dimancheff and Alex Agase but had lost track of many of his former teammates. It was good to see them all once more on the field at Ross-Ade Stadium where, 40 years earlier, they had done something truly special.

The men of the 1943 Purdue football team certainly went on to affect great change in the world. Some, of course, did their part to help win the war with Japan. Many spent decades educating America's youth and imparting on them all of the lessons that the sport of football can teach. Still others went on to impact the business world in various ways. But all were linked back to that one season in the fall of 1943. To a time when the circumstances of the world brought them together. And they learned how to overcome every obstacle on their way to perfection.

Perfect Warriors

FOOTNOTES

Chapter 1

1. "Purdue Adjusting Academic Routine To Military Plan," *Lafayette Journal & Courier*, June 24, 1943.
2. Schott, Tom, ed. *Purdue Football Media Guide (Lafayette: Haywood Printing Co., 2004)*.
3. "1943 Purdue Team Roster", *Purdue Athletics Archives*. Retrieved October 1, 2020.
4. "Purdue At Wisconsin Tomorrow," *Lafayette Journal & Courier*, October 29, 1943.
5. Graham, Gordon. "Graham Crackers," *Lafayette Journal & Courier*, November 1, 1943.
6. "Purdue Beats Wisconsin, 32-0," *Lafayette Journal & Courier*, November 1, 1943.
7. Graham, Gordon. "Graham Crackers," *Lafayette Journal & Courier*, November 1, 1943.
8. "Purdue Beats Wisconsin, 32-0," *Lafayette Journal & Courier*, November 1, 1943.
9. *Ibid.*
10. *Ibid.*
11. "1943 Purdue vs. Wisconsin Box Score," *Purdue Athletics Archives*. Retrieved October 1, 2020.
12. "Irish Are Far Ahead in National Grid Poll," *Indianapolis Star*, November 3, 1943.

Chapter 2

1. "Purdue Points for Wabash in Season Opener," *Lafayette Journal & Courier*, December 5, 1941.
2. "Transcript of Joint Address to Congress Leading to a Declaration of War Against Japan (1941)." *OurDocuments.gov*. https://www.ourdocuments.gov/doc.php?flash=false&doc=73&page=transcript (Retrieved June 14, 2021).
3. "On the Declaration of War with Japan." *Franklin D. Roosevelt Presidential Library and Museum*. http://docs.fdrlibrary.marist.edu/120941.html (Retrieved October 1, 2020).

4. "Purdue Man Hero in Hawaii; Downs Four Jap Planes," *Lafayette Journal & Courier,* December 15, 1941.
5. Sullivan, Patricia. "Obituary, Kenneth Taylor; Pilot Shot Down Planes in Pearl Harbor Attack," *The Washington Post,* December 10, 2006.
6. "Army Flyer Tells of Bagging Four Jap Planes Over Hawaii", *Los Angeles Times,* December 17, 1941.
7. *Ibid.*
8. Gaybreal, Jay. "Two Planes, Eight Guns and Lots of 'Zeros'", *This Week in Army History,* December 7, 2008.
9. "George Welch and his parents meeting Franklin D. Roosevelt at the White House, May 25, 1942." *World War II Database.* https://ww2db.com/image.php?image_id=6335 (Accessed March 18, 2021).
10. "George Welch." *World War II Database.* https://ww2db.com/person_bio.php?person_id=464 (Retrieved March 18, 2021).
11. *Ibid.*
12. "Purdue President Asks Students to 'Keep Chins Up'," *Lafayette Journal & Courier,* December 9, 1941.
13. *Ibid.*
14. Klosson, Ken. "Students Meet in Music Hall to Learn Their Part in War," *Purdue Exponent,* December 16, 1941.
15. *Ibid.*
16. "War Platform (An Editorial)," *Purdue Exponent,* December 9, 1941.
17. "Campus Goes on Full War Time Schedule," *Purdue Exponent,* January 6, 1942.
18. Ibid.
19. Ibid.
20. "Local Draft Board Clarifies Student Rating," *Purdue Exponent,* January 10, 1942
21. Edwards, Willard. "Roosevelt Gets Draft Bill; May Issue Call Oct. 8," *Chicago Tribune,* September 15, 1940.
22. "First Wartime Draft Lottery Since '18 Today," *Chicago Tribune,* March 17, 1942.
23. Vergun, David. "First Peacetime Draft Enacted Just Before World War II," *defense.gov,* April 7, 2020.

https://www.defense.gov/Explore/Features/story/Article/2140942/first-peacetime-draft-enacted-just-before-world-war-ii/ (Retrieved March 24, 2021).
24. "The Draft and World War II," *The National WWII Museum.* https://www.nationalww2museum.org/students-teachers/student-resources/research-starters/draft-and-wwii#:~:text=The%20Draft%20and%20WWII&text=Once%20the%20U.S.%20entered%20WWII,been%20inducted%20in%20the%20military. (Retrieved June 14, 2021).
25. *"Manpower: Sweeping Changes Halt Enlistments, cut Top Draft Age to 38, Give McNutt Selective Service Control." Life. December 21, 1942. p. 27. Retrieved March 24, 2021.*
26. James G. Schneider. *The Navy V-12 Program: Leadership for a Lifetime* (Champaign, Ill.: Marlow Books, 1987), 4-6.
27. Ibid, 6-9.

Chapter 3

1. "Battle of Midway," *history.com,* October 20, 2019. https://www.history.com/topics/world-war-ii/battle-of-midway (Retrieved March 24, 2021).
2. "Battle of Guadalcanal," *history.com,* October 29, 2009. https://www.history.com/topics/world-war-ii/battle-of-guadalcanal (Retrieved March 24, 2021).
3. "Battle of Guadalcanal." *Encyclopedia Britannica,* June 30, 2020. *https://www.britannica.com/event/Battle-of-Guadalcanal* . (Retrieved March 24, 2021).
4. James G. Schneider. *The Navy V-12 Program: Leadership for a Lifetime* (Champaign, Ill.: Marlow Books, 1987), 4-6.
5. Ibid, 2-4.
6. Ibid, 5-6.
7. Ibid.
8. Ibid, 10.
9. Ibid, 11.
10. Ibid, 15-19.
11. Ibid, 14.
12. Ibid, 20.
13. Ibid, 20.
14. "Education and Training: History and Timeline," *U.S. Department of Veteran's Affairs,*

https://www.benefits.va.gov/gibill/history.asp (Retrieved March 24, 2021).
15. Norberg, John. "For 36 Years, Stewart Helped Shape Purdue," *Lafayette Journal & Courier,* June 12, 1988.
16. Schneider. "The Navy V-12 Program,", 68-75.
17. Ibid, 75.
18. Ibid, 98-100.
19. "Executive Order 8802: Prohibition of Discrimination in the Defense Industry," *Roosevelt Library Archives,* http://docs.fdrlibrary.marist.edu/od8802t.html (Retrieved March 24, 2021).
20. Schneider. "The Navy V-12 Program,", 158.
21. Schudel, Matt. "Frederick C. Branch; Was 1st Black Officer in U.S. Marine Corp," *Washington Post,* April 13, 2005.
22. Crave, C.K. "Hamlet's Frederick C. Branch: First African-American office in the Marine Corps," *Richmond Observer,* February 29, 2020.
23. O'Berry, Valerie. "Celebrating the Contributions of Frederick Branch," *United States Marine Corps,* https://www.quantico.marines.mil/News/News-Article-Display/Article/654649/celebrating-the-contributions-of-frederick-branch/ (Retrieved March 24, 2021).
24. Ibid.
25. Ibid.
26. Schneider. "The Navy V-12 Program,", 57-59.
27. Ibid, 253.
28. Ibid, 262-270.

Chapter 4

1. Bartlett, Charles. "Big Ten Charts Course to Take in Army, Navy", *Chicago Tribune,* March 6, 1942.
2. Devine, Tommy. "Big Ten Bosses Plan War-Time Sport Program", *Lafayette Journal & Courier,* March 6, 1942.
3. Ibid.
4. Ibid.

5. Thomas Harbrecht and Robert Barnett. "College Football During World War II: 1941-1945," *Physical Educator*, Vol. 36, Issue 1 (March 1, 1979): 31.
6. "1942 Final AP Football Poll", *College Poll Archive*, http://collegepollarchive.com/football/ap/seasons.cfm?appollid=55#.YGSPuJNKjyw (Retrieved March 31, 2021).
7. "Elward Resigns As Purdue Coach," *Lafayette Journal & Courier*, February 19, 1942.
8. "Purdue Selects Mackey, Burnham," *Lafayette Journal & Courier*, February 26, 1942.
9. Ibid.
10. Schott, Tom, ed. *Purdue Football Media Guide (Lafayette: Haywood Printing Co., 2004)*.
11. Harbrecht and Barnett. "College Football During World War II: 1941-1945," 32-33.
12. Devine, Tommy. "Withdrawal is Granted for Season," *Akron Beacon Journal*, April 7, 1943.
13. "Steeler-Eagle Merger Before Pro League," *Pittsburgh Post-Gazette*, June 17, 1943.
14. Devine, Tommy. "Big-Time Football Alters Pattern; Toughens Men for Armed Forces," *Indianapolis Star*, April 3, 1943.
15. Ibid.
16. "See More Service Teams on Big Ten Gridiron Schedules," *Lafayette Journal & Courier*, May 13, 1943.
17. "Fundamentals Stressed in Spring Grid Practice," *Purdue Exponent*, March 8, 1943.
18. Ibid.
19. "Purdue Grid Clinic Opens Tomorrow; Game Lineups Are Selected by Burnham," *Lafayette Journal & Courier*, April 8, 1943.
20. "Riveters Open Baseball Card with Twin-Bill," *Lafayette Journal & Courier*, April 30, 1943.
21. "Burnham Schedules July Grid Practice," *Purdue Exponent*, May 20, 1943.
22. "Statement of the 1943 Football Season Cancelled," *Michigan State University*, https://onthebanks.msu.edu/Object/162-565-6870/statement-of-the-1943-football-season-cancelled/ (Retrieved March 31, 2021).

23. "Navy Officer Training Course to Bring 1,250 to University," *Lafayette Journal & Courier*, May 7, 1943.

Chapter 5

1. "Irish Given Limbering Up on Scene of Today's Game," *Indianapolis Star*, November 24, 1917.
2. "Hall of Fame: Jim Phelan," *College Football Hall of Fame*, https://footballfoundation.org/hof_search.aspx?hof=1562 *(Retrieved March 31, 2021).*
3. Schott, Tom, ed. *Purdue Football Media Guide* (Lafayette: Haywood Printing Co., 2004).
4. "Hall of Fame: Jim Phelan," *College Football Hall of Fame*, https://footballfoundation.org/hof_search.aspx?hof=1562 *(Retrieved March 31, 2021).*
5. "Rites Tomorrow for Noble Kizer," *Indianapolis Star*, June 14, 1940.
6. Ibid.
7. Campbell, Richard M., ed. *Official 2007 NCAA Division I Football Records Book* (Indianapolis: NCAA, 2007). 76.
8. "Leave Granted Kizer; Aides Will Carry On," *Lafayette Journal & Courier*, August 28, 1937.
9. Schott, Tom, ed. *Purdue Football Media Guide* (Lafayette: Haywood Printing Co., 2004).
10. "Elmer Burnham Will Coach Frosh Gridders at Purdue," *Lafayette Journal & Courier*, May 24, 1935.
11. Ibid.
12. Overaker, Bob. "Elmer Burnham, Builder of Champions, Enters 13th Year at Central High School," *South Bend Tribune*, January 31, 1932.
13. "Former West Newbury Man, Elmer H. Burnham, is Head Football Coach at Purdue," *Newburyport Daily News*, July 2, 1942.
14. "Burnham's Career Topped by '31 State Champions," *South Bend Tribune*, February 26, 1942.
15. "Large Contingent of Soldiers Home," *South Bend Tribune*, January 29, 1919.

16. "Elmer Burnham Named Grid Coach at Purdue," *Kokomo Tribune*, February 26, 1942.
17. Ibid.
18. Ibid.
19. "Burnham's Career Topped by '31 State Champions," *South Bend Tribune*, February 26, 1942.
20. Ibid.
21. Dwyre, Bill and Wharton, David. "The Man, The Legend," *Los Angeles Times*, June 13, 2010.
22. Graham, Gordon. "Graham Crackers," *Lafayette Journal & Courier*, February 26, 1942.
23. "Purdue Selects Mackey, Burnham," *Lafayette Journal & Courier*, February 26, 1942.
24. Ibid.
25. Schott, Tom, ed. *Purdue Football Media Guide (Lafayette: Haywood Printing Co., 2004)*.
26. Devine, Tommy. "Many Radical Changes in Big Ten's Football Pattern," *Lafayette Journal & Courier*, April 3, 1943.
27. "Burnham to Open Spring Football Practice Monday," *Lafayette Journal & Courier*, February 26, 1943.
28. "Riveters Open Baseball Card with Twin-Bill," *Lafayette Journal & Courier*, April 30, 1943.
29. Farmer, Sam. "Hank Stram, 82; Won More Games Than Any Other Coach in the AFL," *Los Angeles Times*, July 5, 2005.
30. "Dutch Fehring Will Report to Navy May 27," *Lafayette Journal & Courier*, April 19, 1943.
31. "Emmett Lowery Leaves for Navy," *Lafayette Journal & Courier*, August 7, 1943.
32. Graham, Gordon. "Graham Crackers," *Lafayette Journal & Courier*, January 6, 1943.
33. "Purdue Mat Coach for 33 Years Dead," *Lafayette Journal & Courier*, June 23, 1973.
34. "Samuel Voinoff," *Lafayette Journal & Courier*, November 18, 1989.
35. Ibid.
36. "Pumas Give Up Football; Dienhart Goes to Purdue as Assistant Coach," *Indianapolis Star*, August 14, 1943.
37. Ibid.

38. Schott, Tom, ed. *Purdue Football Media Guide (Lafayette: Haywood Printing Co., 2004).*
39. Ibid.
40. "Cecil Isbell," *Green Bay Packers,* https://www.packers.com/history/hof/cecil-isbell (Retrieved April 5, 2021)
41. Ibid.
42. Ibid.
43. "Pro Stars Feature Clinic; Over 300 Coaches Attend," *Lafayette Journal & Courier,* April 4, 1942.
44. "Cecil Isbell," *Pro Football Reference,* https://www.pro-football-reference.com/players/I/IsbeCe20.htm (Retrieved April 5, 2021).
45. "Cecil Isbell," *Green Bay Packers,* https://www.packers.com/history/hof/cecil-isbell (Retrieved April 5, 2021)
46. "Coach Lambeau, Still Hopeful of Retaining His Ace Passer, Goes Into Strategic Huddle with Cecil Isbell," *Green Bay Press-Gazette,* July 22, 1943.
47. "Cecil Isbell," *Green Bay Packers,* https://www.packers.com/history/hof/cecil-isbell (Retrieved April 5, 2021)
48. Ibid.

Chapter 6

1. "Navy and Marine Contingents Begin Purdue Training," *Lafayette Journal & Courier,* July 7, 1943.
2. "Riddled Purdue Football Eleven Faces Tough Card," *Lafayette Journal & Courier,* June 28, 1943.
3. "Burnham Calls Purdue Gridmen For First Drill," *Lafayette Journal & Courier,* July 13, 1943.
4. Ibid.
5. "86 Expected to Report to First Football Drill," *Lafayette Journal & Courier,* July 15, 1943.
6. Ibid.
7. Ibid.

8. "1943 Team Roster", *Purdue Athletics Archives,* (Retrieved April 9, 2021).
9. Graham, Gordon. "Graham Crackers," *Lafayette Journal & Courier,* July 17, 1943.
10. "125 Football Prospects Attend Daily Practice," *Purdue Exponent,* July 22, 1943.
11. Graham, Gordon. "Graham Crackers," *Lafayette Journal & Courier,* July 22, 1943.
12. "Gridiron Enthusiasm Pleasing to Burnham," *Purdue Exponent,* July 25, 1943.
13. "86 Expected to Report to First Football Drill," *Lafayette Journal & Courier,* July 15, 1943.
14. Graham, Gordon. "Graham Crackers," *Lafayette Journal & Courier,* August 3, 1943.
15. Roe, Steve, ed. *Iowa Football Media Guide (University of Iowa Athletics: Iowa City, Iowa, 2020).*
16. Davis, Shawn, ed. *Missouri Football Media Guide (Missouri University Athletics: Columbia, Mo., 2020).*
17. Brown, Kent, ed. *Illinois Football Media Guide* (Premier Printing, Champaign, Ill., 2020).
18. Ibid.
19. Ibid.
20. "Young's Yarns," *The Daily Pantagraph,* September 6, 1940.
21. Brown, Kent, ed. *Illinois Football Media Guide* (Premier Printing, Champaign, Ill., 2020).
22. Jauch, Fritz. "Varsity Gridders Battle Frosh Today," *The Daily Illini,* September 19, 1942.
23. Eliot, Ray. "My Greatest Illini Thrill," *The Daily Illini,* April 13, 1944.
24. Walker, Dick. "'Agase For Governor' Illini Road in Dressing Room," *The Daily Illini,* October 11, 1942.
25. Brown, Kent, ed. *Illinois Football Media Guide* (Premier Printing, Champaign, Ill., 2020).
26. "1943 Team Roster", *Purdue Athletics Archives,* (Retrieved April 9, 2021).
27. Graham, Gordon. "Graham Crackers," *Lafayette Journal & Courier,* August 14, 1943.
28. Graham, Gordon. "Graham Crackers," *Lafayette Journal & Courier,* August 5, 1943.

29. Ibid.
30. Ibid.
31. Ibid.
32. Ibid.
33. Graham, Gordon. "Graham Crackers," *Lafayette Journal & Courier*, August 6, 1943.
34. Graham, Gordon. "Graham Crackers," *Lafayette Journal & Courier*, August 12, 1943.
35. Ibid.
36. Graham, Gordon. "Graham Crackers, " *Lafayette Journal & Courier*, August 14, 1943.
37. Ibid.
38. Ibid.
39. Ibid.
40. Ibid.
41. Ibid.

Chapter 7

1. "Detroit University Abandons Football," *Sacramento Bee*, July 19, 1943.
2. "Army's College Soldiers Must Skip Football," *Chicago Tribune*, February 13, 1943.
3. "Carolina May Field Great Grid Squad," *The Daily Tar Heel*, August 4, 1943.
4. "M.S.C. Drops All Athletics For Duration," *Lansing State Journal*, August 11, 1943.
5. Graham, Gordon. "Graham Crackers," *Lafayette Journal & Courier*, August 31, 1943.
6. "Purdue Gridders Ready Today for First Scrimmage," *Lafayette Journal & Courier*, September 2, 1943.
7. "Passing Attack Gives White Team 3 Tallies," *Purdue Exponent*, September 3, 1943.
8. "Purdue Plays Great Lakes Eleven Today," *Chicago Tribune*, September 18, 1943.
9. "Great Lakes to Scrimmage Pros Today," *Chicago Tribune*, September 4, 1943.

10. Smith, Ray. "Grandstand Echoes," *Purdue Exponent*, September 8, 1943.
11. "Football Practice Scheduled Today," *Purdue Exponent*, September 4, 1943.
12. "Flint Back on Purdue Squad," *Lafayette Journal & Courier*, September 15, 1943.
13. "Scrimmage Still Daily Feature in Purdue's Drills," *Lafayette Journal & Courier*, September 7, 1943.
14. Smith, Ray. "Grandstand Echoes," *Purdue Exponent*, September 8, 1943.
15. "Burnham Sends Squad Through Secret Drill," *Purdue Exponent*, September 16, 1943.
16. Graham, Gordon. "Graham Crackers," *Lafayette Journal & Courier*, September 13, 1943.
17. "Purdue Squad Drills Inside," *Lafayette Journal & Courier*, September 14, 1943.
18. Graham, Gordon. "Graham Crackers," *Lafayette Journal & Courier*, September 16, 1943.
19. "Purdue Gridders Leave Today for Great Lakes," *Lafayette Journal & Courier*, September 17, 1943.
20. Ibid.
21. "Killed in Crash," *Chicago Tribune*, September 18, 1943.

Chapter 8

1. "Fifty-Three Candidates Attend Hilltop Workout," *Kenosha News*, August 31, 1943.
2. "Purdue, Marquette Near Important Grid Struggle," *Lafayette Journal & Courier*, September 23, 1943.
3. Ibid.
4. "Team Given Big Send-Off from Station," *Purdue Exponent*, September 26, 1943.
5. "Combs Captain," *Lafayette Journal & Courier*, September 23, 1943.
6. Graham, Gordon. "Graham Crackers," *Lafayette Journal & Courier*, September 27, 1943.
7. Ibid.
8. Fraley, Oscar. "Purdue 1st in Midwest," *Lafayette Journal & Courier* September 27, 1943.

Chapter 9

1. Schott, Tom, ed. *Purdue Football Media Guide* (Lafayette: Haywood Printing Co., 2004).
2. "New Grid Rivalry Trophy is at Stake Here Saturday," *Lafayette Journal & Courier*, September 28, 1943.
3. Walker, Dick. "The Bull Pen," *The Daily Illini*, May 22, 1943.
4. Schmelzle, Bill. "Agase, Butkovich Toast Illinois Gridders," *The Daily Illini*, July 1, 1943.
5. Graham, Gordon. "Graham Crackers," *Lafayette Journal & Courier*, September 28, 1943.
6. Schmelzle, Bill. "Illini Polish 'T' for Wisconsin Grid Fracas," *The Daily Illini*, October 6, 1943.
7. Drum, Jill. "Five New Men Join Illini Gridders for Purdue Game," *The Daily Illini*, September 29, 1943.
8. Graham, Gordon. "Graham Crackers," *Lafayette Journal & Courier*, September 28, 1943.
9. Ibid.
10. Ibid.
11. Smith, Ray. "Grandstand Echoes," *Purdue Exponent*, October 5, 1943.
12. Peabody, Bob. "'Good Friend but Tough Enemy!' Illini Praise Ex-Mate Tony Butkovich," *That Daily Illini*, October 3, 1943.
13. Ibid.
14. Schmelzle, Bill. "A Happy Illini Gang Gets Together with Purdue," *The Daily Illini*, October 3, 1943.
15. Ibid.
16. Ibid.

Chapter 10

1. "Atwood Center," *atwoodpark.org*, https://atwoodpark.org/about (Retrieved May 21, 2021).
2. Garcia, J. Malcolm. "German POWs on the American Homefront", *Smithsonian Magazine*, https://www.smithsonianmag.com/history/german-pows-

on-the-american-homefront-141009996 (Retrieved May 21, 2021).
3. Devine, Tommy. "Camp Grant and Illinois to Open Football Schedule Tomorrow at Champaign," *Freeport Journal-Standard*, September 10, 1943.
4. "Soldier Giants Here Saturday," *Lafayette Journal & Courier*, October 5, 1943.
5. Claasen, Harold. "Notre Dame 1st in Gridiron Poll," *Indianapolis Star*, October 6, 1943.
6. "Prepares for Soldiers," *Indianapolis Star*, October 5, 1943.
7. Graham, Gordon. "Graham Crackers," *Lafayette Journal & Courier*, October 11, 1943.
8. Ibid.
9. Claasen, Harold. "Purdue Leaps to 5th Place," *Lafayette Journal & Courier*, October 12, 1943.

Chapter 11

1. "Hall of Fame Veterans" *Baseball Hall of Fame*, https://baseballhall.org/discover-more/stories/hall-of-famer-facts/hall-of-fame-veterans (Retrieved May 21, 2021).
2. Chesterton, Eric. "The Time Spring Training Didn't Go South," *Major League Baseball*, March 4, 2020. https://www.mlb.com/news/spring-training-during-wwii (Retrieved Mar 21, 2021).
3. Ibid.
4. Ibid.
5. Ibid.
6. "Lou Boudreau Here; Tribe In First Workout Tuesday," *Lafayette Journal & Courier*, March 15, 1943.
7. "Indians Thump Riveters 12-3," *Lafayette Journal & Courier*, April 1, 1943.
8. Basford, Mike and Emig, Jerry, eds. *2020 Ohio State Football Media Guide*. https://ohiostatebuckeyes.com/wp-content/uploads/2020/10/2020FBMediaGuide-3.pdf (Retrieved May 21, 2021).
9. Ibid.
10. Schlemmer, Jim. "Bucks Not Too Bad," *Akron Beacon Journal*, September 15, 1943.

11. Perkins, Glen. "Name Burnham Coach of Week," *Lafayette Journal & Courier*, October 14, 1943.
12. Ibid.
13. "Rivals Clash in Cleveland's Spacious Municipal Stadium," *Lafayette Journal & Courier*, October 15, 1943.
14. "Ernie Parks Takes Oath," *The Lantern*, October 8, 1943.
15. Graham, Gordon. "Graham Crackers," *Lafayette Journal & Courier*, October 18, 1943.

Chapter 12

1. Claasen, Howard. "Notre Dame Far Ahead in National Gridiron Poll; Purdue Ranks Fifth," *Indianapolis Star*, October 12, 1943.
2. Roe, Steven, Wagner, Traci and Weitzel, Matt, eds. *2020 Iowa Football Media Guide*. https://hawkeyesports.com/2020-media-guide-2/ (Retrieved May 24, 2021).
3. "They Started Here: Eddie Anderson," *Globe Gazette*, April 20, 1940.
4. O'Leary, Josh. "The Forgotten Hawks," *Iowa Magazine*, November 2017. https://magazine.foriowa.org/archive/archive-story.php?ed=true&storyid=1682 (Retrieved May 24, 2021).
5. "SUI's Nile Kinnick Dies in Action," *The Daily Iowan*, June 5, 1943.
6. Mosely, Claire. "Out of Bounds," *Iowa City Press-Citizen*, July 2, 1943.
7. McCutcheon, John. "'Purdue Et Al' is Making a Grand Record; 'Purdue Says: War is Helpful'" *Chicago Tribune*, October 17, 1943.
8. Graham, Gordon. "Graham Crakers," *Lafayette Journal & Courier*, October 20, 1943.
9. Graham, Gordon. "Graham Crackers," *Lafayette Journal & Courier*, October 25, 1943.
10. "Bertelli, Daley Among Those Leaving Football Fields Nov. 1," *Lafayette Journal & Courier*, October 23, 1943.

11. Graham, Gordon. "Graham Crackers," *Lafayette Journal & Courier*, October 25, 1943.
12. "Unbeaten Riveters in Homecoming Tilt," *Lafayette Journal & Courier*, October 22, 1943.
13. Claussen, Harold. "Purdue Holds Fourth Place," *Lafayette Journal & Courier*, October 26, 1943.
14. Smith, Wilfred. "Butkovich and Frickey Given Marine Orders," *Chicago Tribune*, October 27, 1943.

Chapter 13

1. Graham, Gordon. "Graham Crackers," *Lafayette Journal & Courier*, October 27, 1943.
2. Smith, Wilfred. "Butkovich and Frickey Given Marine Orders," *Chicago Tribune*, October 27, 1943.
3. Graham, Gordon. "Graham Crackers," *Lafayette Journal & Courier*, October 27, 1943.
4. Ibid.
5. "Skeleton Purdue Squad Drills for Wisconsin Fray Saturday," *Lafayette Journal & Courier*, October 28, 1943.
6. Ibid.
7. Roberts, Glenn. "Butkovich Visits Eliot as Illini Drill for Michigan," *The Daily Illini*, October 28, 1943.
8. Ibid.
9. Ibid.
10. Ibid.
11. Ibid.
12. Graham, Gordon. "Graham Crackers," *Lafayette Journal & Courier*, October 25, 1943.
13. "Explosive Tony Leading Big Ten," *Lafayette Journal & Courier*, October 28, 1943.
14. Graham, Gordon. "Graham Crackers," *Lafayette Journal & Courier*, October 29, 1943.
15. "Skeleton Purdue Squad Drills for Wisconsin Fray Saturday," *Lafayette Journal & Courier*, October 28, 1943.
16. Ibid.
17. "The Edgewater Beach Hotel: Magic By the Lake," *WTTW*, https://interactive.wttw.com/a/chicago-stories-edgewater-beach-hotel (Retrieved May 25, 2021).

18. Graham, Gordon. "Graham Crackers," *Lafayette Journal & Courier,* November 1, 1943.
19. Ibid.
20. Graham, Gordon. "Graham Crackers," *Lafayette Journal & Courier,* November 2, 1943.
21. Ibid.
22. Ibid.
23. Ibid.

Chapter 14

1. "Irish Are Far Ahead in National Grid Poll," *Indianapolis Star,* November 3, 1943.
2. "Burnham Must Replace 13 Men in Two Days of Drill," *Lafayette Journal & Courier,* November 2, 1943.
3. "Return of Purdue Players Awaited," *Indianapolis Star,* November 2, 1943.
4. Swanson, Bernard. "Bill Daley Goes to Michigan in Gopher Sports Exodus," *Minneapolis Morning Tribune,* July 7, 1943.
5. Rovnak, Paul and Tibbitts, Ryan. *2020 Minnesota Football Media Guide.* https://gophersports.com/documents/2020/10/14/2020_Football_Media_Guide_WEB.pdf (Retrieved May 25, 2021).
6. "Iowa City Speculates Over Grid Successor to Bierman," *Minneapolis Morning Tribune,* May 12, 1943.
7. "Dimancheff is Grid Surprise," *Lafayette Journal & Courier,* November 3, 1943.
8. "Burnham Must Replace 13 Men in Two Days of Drill," *Lafayette Journal & Courier,* November 2, 1943.
9. "Dick Barwegen Will Captain Purdue Team in Minnesota and Indiana Games," *Lafayette Journal & Courier,* November 4, 1943.
10. Ibid.
11. Graham, Gordon. "Graham Crackers," *Lafayette Journal & Courier,* November 4, 1943.
12. "Weather Today Big Concern for Gophers, Purdue," *Minneapolis Morning Tribune,* November 6, 1943.

13. Ibid.
14. Hall, Halsey. "Gophers Ask 'How Did it Happen'? Lose Five Key Men in Four Tilts," *Minneapolis Star,* November 8, 1943.
15. "Superstars: Verne Gagne," *WWE.* <https://www.wwe.com/superstars/verne-gagne> (Retrieved May 26, 2021).
16. "Five Die as Snowstorm Ties Up Whole State," *Minneapolis Star,* November 8, 1943.
17. Claasen, Harold. "Great Notre Dame Team Sweeps Poll; Purdue 2nd," *Lafayette Journal & Courier,* November 9, 1943.

Chapter 15

1. "Grid Standings," *Lafayette Journal & Courier,* November 16, 1943.
2. "Revamp Purdue Outfit for I.U.," *Lafayette Journal & Courier,* November 16, 1943.
3. "Purdue Gridders In Monday Layoff," *Lafayette Journal & Courier,* November 9, 1943.
4. "4 From Notre Dame, Pete Pihos of Indiana Honored by Colliers," *Indianapolis Star,* December 10, 1943.
5. Chamberlain, Charles. "3 Tough Games Facing Lujack," *Ironwood Daily Globe,* November 9, 1943.
6. Schott, Tom, ed. *Purdue Football Media Guide (Lafayette: Haywood Printing Co., 2004).*
7. "The Old Oaken Bucket," *All Poetry* <https://allpoetry.com/Samuel-Woodworth> (Retrieved May 27, 2021).
8. "Purdue Eleven Works Indoors," *Lafayette Journal & Courier,* November 10, 1943.
9. "Barwegen to Lead Purdue," *Lafayette Journal & Courier,* November 18, 1943.
10. "McMillan Orders Secret Practice," *Indianapolis Star,* November 16, 1943.
11. "Burnham Has Men Hustling," *Lafayette Journal & Courier,* November 17, 1943.
12. "Fifteen Are Killed in Crash of Speeding Football Train," *Indianapolis Morning Star,* November 1, 1903.
13. Ibid.

14. Gugin, Linda. *The Governors of Indiana.* (Indianapolis: Indiana Historical Society Press, 2006).
15. "Purdue Team Will Not Pass Scenes of Last Year's Disaster," *Indianapolis Morning Star,* November 11, 1904.
16. "Forecast for Today," *Indianapolis Star*, November 20, 1943.

Chapter 16

1. Claassen, Harold. "Irish Tighten Grip on National Title," *Indianapolis Star,* November 22, 1943.
2. Meyer, Bob. "Great Lakes Upsets Irish, 19-14," *Indianapolis Star*, November 29, 1943.
3. Ibid.
4. Ibid.
5. Claassen, Harold. "Purdue Fifth in Nation in Poll," *Lafayette Journal & Courier*, November 30, 1943.
6. Dyer, Braven. "Trojan Aerial Attack Beats Huskies, 29-0," *Los Angeles Times,*
7. Hoff, Dave. "Purdue Leads AP Big Ten Team with Three Named," *Lafayette Journal & Courier, November 30, 1943.*
8. "Barwegen Named Most Valuable," *Lafayette Journal & Courier, November 30, 1943.*
9. Schott, Tom, ed. *Purdue Football Media Guide (Lafayette: Haywood Printing Co., 2004).*
10. Graham, Gordon. "Graham Crackers," *Lafayette Journal & Courier*, April 17, 1944.
11. "Burnham Resigns at Purdue," *Lafayette Journal & Courier,* May 15, 1944.
12. Ibid.
13. Graham, Gordon. "Graham Crackers," *Lafayette Journal & Courier,* May 15, 1944.
14. Ibid.
15. O'Donnell, Dennis. *Rochester Football 2020-21.* https://indd.adobe.com/view/539eab90-1ffe-475f-a298-fd8c5412acaa (Retrieved June 2, 2021).
16. "Burnham Resigns at Purdue," *Lafayette Journal & Courier,* May 15, 1944.

17. "Cecil Isbell Purdue Head Coach," *Lafayette Journal & Courier*, May 16, 1943.
18. Adams, Edwin. 1949 *Baltimore Colts Press – Radio – Television Guide.* https://res.cloudinary.com/nflclubs/image/upload/colts/m71bl6tcbhmdoxeuup00.pdf (Retrieved June 2, 2021).
19. Ibid.
20. McIver, Stuart. "Driskell, New Colts Coach, Holds Drill," *Baltimore Sun*, September 20, 1943.
21. Prell, Edward. "Lambeau Leaves Packers for Cardinals; Wants Isbell as Aid," *Chicago Tribune*, February 2, 1950.
22. "Ex-Purdue, Colts' Coach Cecil Isbell Dies at 69," *Lafayette Journal & Courier*, June 25, 1985.
23. Ibid.
24. Norberg, John. "Joe Dienhart: 1903-1987," *Lafayette Journal & Courier*, December 9, 1987.
25. Henderson, Pat. *1988 Purdue Men's and Women's Golf Media Guide.* Purdue Athletics.
26. White, Sara. *2008 Purdue Men's Gold Media Guide.* Purdue Athletics.
27. Ibid.
28. "Sam Voinoff," *Lafayette Journal & Courier,* November 18, 1989.
29. Ramey, Bruce. "Red Mackey Dies; Served Purdue Sports for 46 of His 65 Years," *Lafayette Journal & Courier*, February 23, 1971.
30. Ibid.
31. "Purdue's Ward Lambert, Hall of Fame Coach, Dies at 69," *Lafayette Journal & Courier*, January 20, 1958.
32. Ibid.
33. Ibid.
34. Ibid.
35. "Purdue Mat Coach For 33 Years Dead," *Lafayette Journal & Courier*, June 23, 1973.
36. Ibid.
37. Ibid.
38. Ibid.

Chapter 17

1. Schott, Tom, ed. *Purdue Football Media Guide (Lafayette: Haywood Printing Co., 2004).*
2. "Purdue at Michigan Tomorrow," *Lafayette Journal & Courier,* October 27, 1944.
3. "Associated Press All-Big Ten," *Lafayette Journal & Courier,* November 27, 1944.
4. "Dimancheff Fullback on New York Sun All-America Team," *Lafayette Journal & Courier,* December 4, 1944.
5. "Boris 'Babe' Dimancheff Named Most Valuable Player on Purdue's Eleven," *Lafayette Journal & Courier,* November 28, 1944.
6. Segreti, James. "Fenger Whips Leo, 18-0, for City Prep Title," *Chicago Tribune,* December 1, 1940.
7. Adams, Edwin. *1949 Baltimore Colts Press – Radio – Television Guide.* https://res.cloudinary.com/nflclubs/image/upload/colts/m71bl6tcbhmdoxeuup00.pdf (Retrieved June 2, 2021).
8. Ibid.
9. "N.Y. Yanks Get Barwegen," *Lafayette Journal & Courier,* January 31, 1947.
10. McIver, Stuart. "Barwegan Called Key Player in Colts' Drive for Title," *Baltimore Sun,* November 27, 1948.
11. "Dick Barwegen," *Pro Football Reference,* https://www.pro-football-reference.com/players/B/BarwDi00.htm (Retrieved June 3, 2021).
12. "Barwegen Goes to Bears in Deal," *Baltimore Sun,* September 8, 1950.
13. "Dick Barwegen," *Pro Football Reference,* https://www.pro-football-reference.com/players/B/BarwDi00.htm (Retrieved June 3, 2021).
14. "Barwegen Dies; Former Bear, Colt," *Chicago Tribune,* September 4, 1966.
15. Ibid.
16. "Eddie Cycenas Reported Dead," *Lafayette Journal & Courier,* October 12, 1945.

17. Dukehart, Thomas. *1948 Baltimore Colts Press – Radio – Television Guide.* https://res.cloudinary.com/nflclubs/image/upload/colts/ssgpevzyfmkbyh5unbp8.pdf (Retrieved June 3, 2021).
18. "Louis DeFilippo" *Fordham Athletics Hall of Fame.* https://fordhamsports.com/honors/hall-of-fame/louis-defilippo/84 (Retrieved June 3, 2021).
19. "Valley Mourns Loss of DeFilippo," *New Haven Register,* March 11, 2000.
20. Schott, Tom, ed. *Purdue Football Media Guide (Lafayette: Haywood Printing Co., 2004).*
21. Ibid.
22. "Babe Dimancheff," *Pro Football Reference.* https://www.pro-football-reference.com/players/D/DimaBa20.htm (Retrieved June 3, 2021).
23. "Babe Dimancheff," *Purdue Athletics Hall of Fame.* https://purduesports.com/news/2009/2/9/2009_Hall_Of_Fame.aspx (Retrieved June 3, 2021).
24. "Stanley Dubicki," *South Bend Tribune,* September 13, 2012.
25. "Bump Elliott Named Athletic Director," *Iowa City Press-Citizen,* June 11, 1970.
26. Ibid.
27. Ibid.
28. Leistikow, Chad. "'A True Gentleman'," *Iowa City Press-Citizen,* December 10, 2019.
29. Ibid.
30. Ibid.
31. Ibid.
32. Ibid.
33. "Big Ten Medal to Tom Hughes," *Lafayette Journal & Courier,* June 24, 1946.
34. "Tom Hughes Dies; Was Football Star, Coach," *St. Louis Post-Dispatch,* March 30, 1980.
35. "Former Purdue Athletic Trainer Pinky Newell Dies," *Lafayette Journal & Courier,* October 16, 1984.
36. Ibid.
37. Ibid.
38. "Keith Parker" *St. Louis Post-Dispatch,* April 10, 2007.

39. "VU Loses, Hobart Here Tuesday," *Vidette-Messenger of Porter County*, October 21, 1946.
40. "Ex-Councilman Vacanti Dies," *Lincoln Journal Star*, November 18, 1981.
41. "AP All-Big 6 Teams List Five Cornhusker Players," November 29, 1946.
42. Adams, Edwin. 1949 *Baltimore Colts Press – Radio – Television Guide*. https://res.cloudinary.com/nflclubs/image/upload/colts/m71bl6tcbhmdoxeuup00.pdf (Retrieved June 2, 2021).
43. "Ex-Councilman Vacanti Dies," *Lincoln Journal Star*, November 18, 1981.
44. Ibid.
45. Ibid.

Chapter 18

1. Jauch, Fritz. "Phillip, Agase, Genis, Baumann Back on Campus," *The Daily Illini*, April 26, 1946.
2. Graham, Gordon. "Graham Crackers," *Lafayette Journal & Courier*, October 6, 1946.
3. Ibid.
4. Ibid.
5. Ibid.
6. Peasley, Don. "Cecil Isbell Bemoans Injuries; Eliot Praises Dike's Punting," *The Daily Illini*, October 6, 1946.
7. Ibid.
8. Ibid.
9. Ibid.
10. Smith, Wilfred. "Illini Whip U.C.L.A. in Rose Bowl, 45-14," *Chicago Tribune*, January 2, 1947.
11. Condon, David. "Ray Eliot Was a Big Winner in Every Respect," *Chicago Tribune*, February 25, 1980.
12. Brown, Kent, ed. *Illinois Football Media Guide* (Premier Printing, Champaign, Ill., 2020).
13. Jones, William K. "A Brief History of the 6th Marines," *United States Marine Corps.*,

https://www.usmcu.edu/Portals/218/A%20Brief%20History%20of%20the%20206th%20Marines%20%20PCN%20201900310000.pdf (Retrieved June 7, 2021).
14. "The Last Game – Survival," *Lafayette Journal & Courier*, February 9, 1986.
15. Ibid.
16. Ibid.
17. Ibid.
18. "Notes on Meanderings of Vanished Illini," *The Daily Illini*, January 17, 1945.
19. Jones, William K. "A Brief History of the 6th Marines," *United States Marine Corps.*, https://www.usmcu.edu/Portals/218/A%20Brief%20History%20of%20the%20206th%20Marines%20%20PCN%20201900310000.pdf (Retrieved June 7, 2021).
20. Ruester, Lynn. "Off the Cuff," *The Evening Courier*, July 26, 1945.
21. Jones, William K. "A Brief History of the 6th Marines," *United States Marine Corps.*, https://www.usmcu.edu/Portals/218/A%20Brief%20History%20of%20the%20206th%20Marines%20%20PCN%20201900310000.pdf (Retrieved June 7, 2021).
22. Ibid.
23. Jauch, Fritz. "The Morning After," *The Daily Illini*, June 27, 1946.
24. Brooks, Jim. "Babbling Brooks," *The Daily Illini*, May 28, 1947.
25. "The Last Game – Survival," *Lafayette Journal & Courier*, February 9, 1986.
26. Doherty, Bob. "Kasap Watches Grid Practice," *The Daily Illini*, August 2, 1945.
27. Doherty, Bob. "Time Out…," *The Daily Illini*, December 13, 1945.
28. Jauch, Fritz. "1946 Illinois Football Squad Opens Drills Monday," *The Daily Illini*, August 17, 1946.
29. "Kasap Signs with Cleveland Browns," *The Daily Illini*, January 23, 1947.
30. "Colts Make Player Deals," *Baltimore Sun*, August 27, 1947.
31. "Betty Ann Kasap,"

32. Jauch, Fritz. "1946 Illinois Football Squad Opens Drills Monday," *The Daily Illini*, August 17, 1946.
33. Gary, Alex. "Unlikely Star Joe Buscemi, Part of College Football's Biggest Turnaround," *Rockford Register Star*, https://www.rrstar.com/story/sports/2020/08/31/unlikely-star-joe-buscemi-part-of-college-footballrsquos-greatest-turnaround/42797021/ (Retrieved June 8, 2021).
34. "Joseph Buscemi," *Cleveland Jewish News*, May 6, 2009.
35. "Bauman and Dimancheff Placed on Big Ten Team," *Lafayette Journal & Courier*, November 22, 1944.
36. Lucas, Brian, ed. *2020 Wisconsin Football Fact Book*. https://uwbadgers.com/documents/2020/10/19/2020_Wisconsin_Football_Fact_Book.pdf (Retrieved June 8, 2021).
37. "The Last Game – Survival," *Lafayette Journal & Courier*, February 9, 1986.
38. "Bauman, U.W. Tackle in '42, Killed by Japs," *Wisconsin State Journal*, June 6, 1945.
39. Larkin, Will and Bannon, Tim. "The 32 Greatest Illinois High School Football Teams of All Time," *Chicago Tribune*, November 17, 2017.
40. "Former Thornton Coach to Receive Recognition," *Chicago Tribune*, May 7, 1983.
41. "Battle of Peleliu Facts," *World War II Facts*. http://www.worldwar2facts.org/battle-of-peleliu-facts.html (Retrieved June 8, 2021).
42. Nichols, Charles and Shaw, Henry. *Okinawa: Victory in the Pacific*. (U.S. Marine Corps, Government Printing Office, 1955).
43. Ibid.
44. Morrow, Joseph. "Illinois Yanks' 'Snake Hunt' Bags 180 Japs," *Chicago Tribune*, May 18, 1945.
45. Ruester, Lynn. "Agase Wounded on Okinawa," *The Evening Courier*, July 13, 1945.
46. Ibid.
47. Smith, Wilfred. "Colleges Have Greatest Year for Football," *Chicago Tribune*, December 22, 1946.
48. Schott, Tom, ed. *Purdue Football Media Guide* (Lafayette: Haywood Printing Co., 2004).

49. Schlemmer, Jim. "Cleveland Browns, 48-Strong, to Face Free-for-All Fight," *Akron Beacon Journal*, July 27, 1948.
50. "Year by Year Season Results," *Cleveland Browns*. <u>https://www.clevelandbrowns.com/team/history/year-by-year-results</u> *(Retrieved June 9, 2021)*.
51. "Agase is Traded to Dallas 11," *Akron Beacon Journal*, May 13, 1952.
52. Cromie, Robert. "Alex Agase to Join N.U. Coaching Staff," *Chicago Tribune*, January 20, 1956.
53. Condon, David. "In the Wake of the News," *Chicago Tribune*, December 19, 1963.
54. Damer, Roy. "Alex Agase is New Purdue Coach," *Chicago Tribune*, December 16, 1972.
55. Ibid.
56. Schott, Tom, ed. *Purdue Football Media Guide (Lafayette: Haywood Printing Co., 2004)*.
57. Ibid.
58. McCabe, Mick. "AD Agase Calls It Quits, Stunning EMU," *Detroit Free Press*, May 7, 1982.
59. Saylor, Jack. "Triple Glory," *Detroit Free Press*, November 3, 1982.
60. Thompson, Ken. "Boilermaker Hall of Famer Agase Dies," *Lafayette Journal & Courier*, May 5, 2007.
61. Kindred, Randy. "Two Area Products Among 25 on Illini's 'All-Century' Squad," *The Pantagraph*, November 2, 1990.
62. Thompson, Ken. "Agase Fondly Recalls Perfect Season in '43," *Lafayette Journal & Courier*, November 1, 2001.
63. Ibid.
64. Thompson, Ken. "Boilermaker Hall of Famer Agase Dies," *Lafayette Journal & Courier*, May 5, 2007.

Chapter 19

1. Ruester, Lynn. "Off the Cuff," *The Daily Illini*, May 23, 1945.
2. "Illini Gridders 'Play' with Marines," *The Daily Illini*, January 7, 1944.
3. "Tony Butkovich, Hero of Local Boy, Killed by Sniper on Okinawa Island," *Richmond Palladium-Item*, May 6, 1945.
4. Ibid.

5. Ibid.
6. Ruester, Lynn. "Off the Cuff," *The Evening Courier*, April 18, 1945.
7. Nichols, Charles and Shaw, Henry. *Okinawa: Victory in the Pacific*. (U.S. Marine Corps, Government Printing Office, 1955).
8. Ibid.
9. Ibid.
10. Ibid.
11. Ibid.
12. "Tony Butkovich is Killed on Okinawa," *The Moline Dispatch*, May 5, 1945.
13. Ibid.
14. Ibid.
15. Ibid.
16. "Battle of Okinawa in Color," *Smithsonian Channel*. https://www.smithsonianchannel.com/details/show/battle-of-okinawa-in-color (Retrieved June 9, 2021).
17. "Battle of Okinawa," *history.com*, October 29, 2009. https://www.history.com/topics/world-war-ii/battle-of-guadalcanal (Retrieved June 11, 2021).
18. "Cpl. Tony Butkovich Killed on Okinawa," *The Daily Illini*, May 5, 1945.
19. Graham, Gordon. "Graham Crackers," *Lafayette Journal & Courier*, May 14, 1945.
20. Connor, Joseph. "A Grave Task: The Wartime Job Nobody Wanted," *HistoryNet*, https://www.historynet.com/grave-task-men-buried-wartime-dead.htm (Retrieved June 11, 2021).
21. "Tony Butkovich's Body Returned from Pacific," *Decatur Herald*, June 10, 1949.

Afterword

1. "Men Outnumber Co-eds 5-to-1 As Purdue Enrollment Grows," *Lafayette Journal & Courier*, September 15, 1939.
2. "Purdue Enrollment Promises to Come Close to 1939 Mark," *Lafayette Journal & Courier*, September 16, 1940.

3. "Purdue Enrollment 14,240; Fewer Veterans in School," *Lafayette Journal & Courier,* October 17, 1949.
4. Ibid.
5. "Cradle of Astronauts," *Purdue University.* https://www.purdue.edu/space/astronauts.php (Retrieved June 11, 2021).
6. James G. Schneider. *The Navy V-12 Program: Leadership for a Lifetime* (Champaign, Ill.: Marlow Books, 1987), 324.
7. Ibid, 342-354.
8. Ibid, 470-471.
9. "40th Reunion: The 9-0 1943 Boilermakers," *The Boilermaker.* (Lafayette: Haywood Printing Co., 1983).
10. Milauskas, Leonard. Interview by Cory Palm, April 17, 2007.

ABOUT THE AUTHOR

Cory Palm is currently the Director of Broadcast Services for Purdue Athletics and has worked in and around the football program since 2004. He holds a B.A in Journalism from Michigan State University and an M.A. in Public Relations and Sport Management from Purdue. He became aware of Tony Butkovich and the rest of the 1943 Boilermakers while researching Purdue scoring records in 2006. In 2018, he produced a documentary on the *Perfect Warriors* that has aired more than a dozen times on B1G Network and is available on B1G+.
Originally from rural Illinois, Cory now lives in Lafayette, Ind., with his wife Jaclyn and his daughter Alyssa.

Made in the USA
Monee, IL
04 January 2023